My Big Book of NUMBERS, LETTERS & WORDS

NUMBER GAMES 1-70

Table of Contents

To parents: NUMBER GAMES 1-70

In this section, your child will complete activities designed to enhance number recitation and number recognition skills. On the front of each page, your child will complete enjoyable number puzzles, connecting numbered dots in order while reciting each number aloud. On the back of each page, your child will color pictures by number, to reinforce his or her number recognition skills, while developing fine motor skills.

These activities will help your child develop confidence in his or her ability to recite and recognize numbers from 1 to 70. This confidence will lead to your child's smooth progress in other number skill areas such as addition.

The activities in this section will help your child build a foundation for future math learning. If your child is ready to advance to the next skill after completing this section, please refer to the appropriate book from our other Math Skills products for further work.

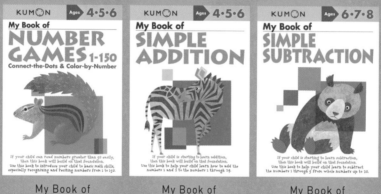

My Book of
NUMBER GAMES 1-150

My Book of
SIMPLE ADDITION

My Book of
SIMPLE SUBTRACTION

How to hold a pencil properly

There are several ways to teach children to hold a pencil properly.
Here is one example.

1 Help your child form an "L" shape with his or her thumb and forefinger as pictured here. Place the pencil against the top of the bent middle finger and on the thumb joint.

2 Now, have your child squeeze the pencil with the thumb and forefinger.

3 Check the way that your child is holding the pencil against the picture to decide whether or not it is the proper way.

It can be difficult for a child who does not yet have enough strength in his or her hand and fingers to hold the pencil properly. Please teach this skill gradually, so that your child will remaln interested and willing to hold a pencil naturally.

In this section, the following 8 colored crayons are used. Please provide them for your child.

red   orange   yellow   green   blue   violet(purple)   brown   black

Let's Eat!

Name

Date

To parents Guide your child to write his or her name and date in the box above. Enjoyable connect-the-dots activities are on odd-numbered pages. It is okay if your child draws shaky lines at first; his or her fine motor skills will improve. Ask your child to guess what is shown in the picture. (The answers are at the end of this section.) For extra fun, your child can also color the pictures.

■ Draw a line from I to I0 in order while saying each number.

What is it?

To parents On even-numbered pages are color-by-number activities. If your child has difficulty finding the numbers, please point them out. Praise your child as he or she finishes each activity.

■ Use the key below to color by number.
 I = yellow

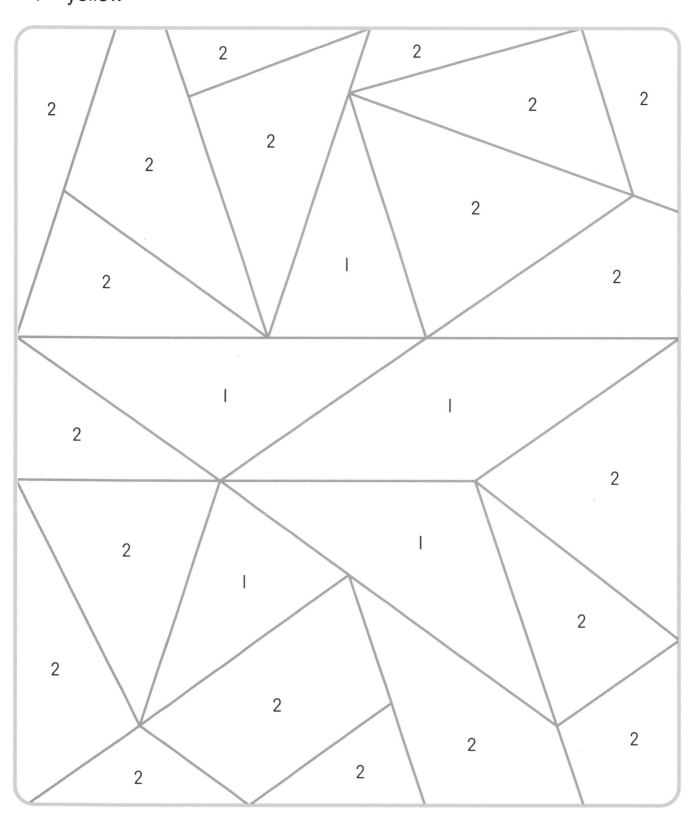

2 My Own Place

Name
Date

■ Draw a line from 1 to 10 in order while saying each number.

5

What is it?

■ Use the key below to color by number.
  3 = brown   4 = orange

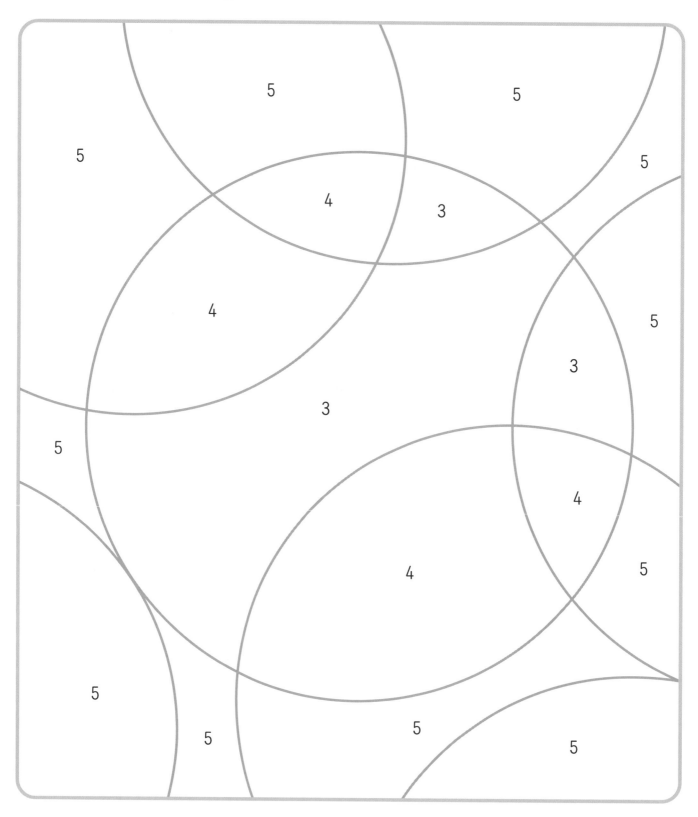

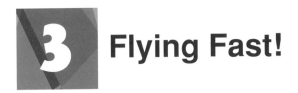
3 Flying Fast!

■ Draw a line from 1 to 10 in order while saying each number.

What is it?

■ Use the key below to color by number.
6 = green   7 = yellow

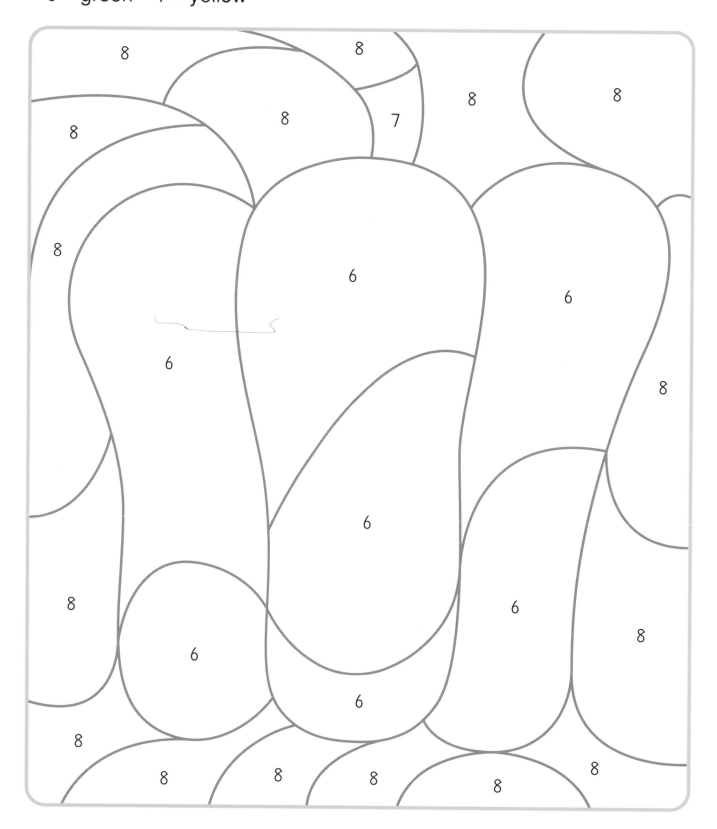

Ka-boom!

Name

Date

■ Draw a line from 1 to 15 in order while saying each number.

What is it?

■ Use the key below to color by number.
   11 = brown   12 = yellow

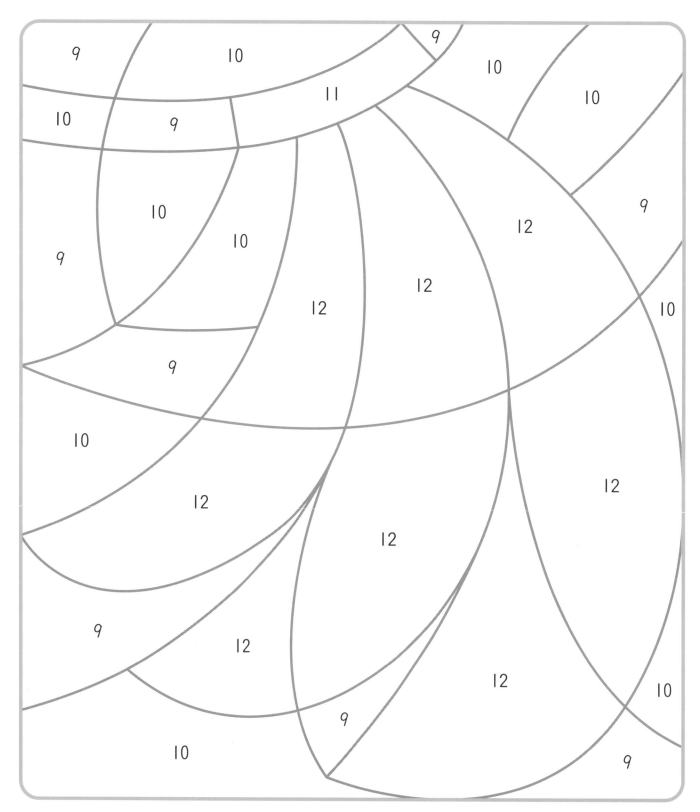

Whoosh

To parents On this page, your child will have to draw a line that will cross another line. If your child has difficulty finding the next number, please point it out for him or her. Please praise your child as he or she finishes each activity.

■ Draw a line from 1 to 15 in order while saying each number.

What is it?

■ Use the key below to color by number.
13 = brown   14 = orange

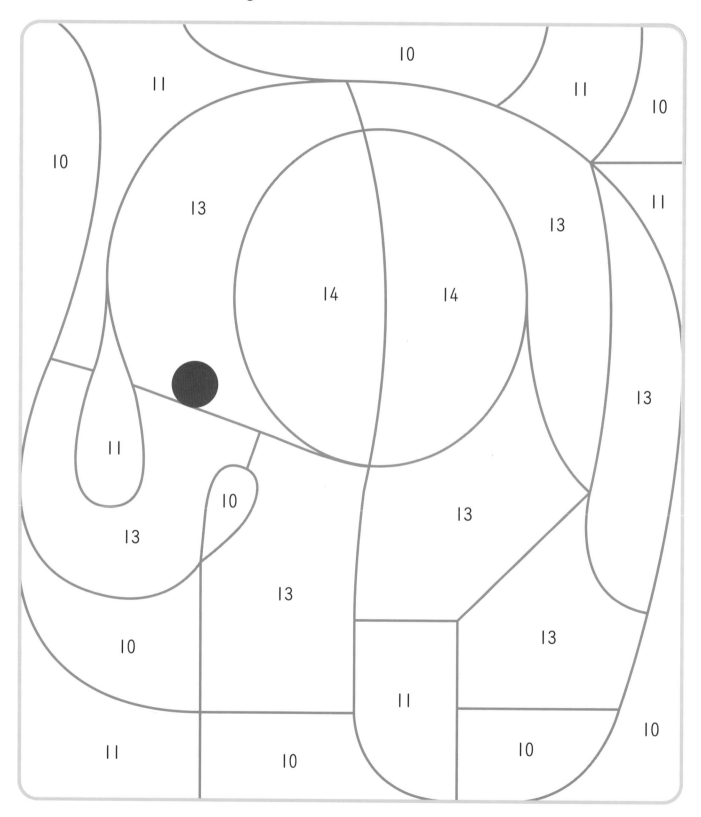

6 Camping

Name

Date

■ Draw a line from 1 to 15 in order while saying each number.

What is it?

- Use the key below to color by number.
  14 = orange   15 = red

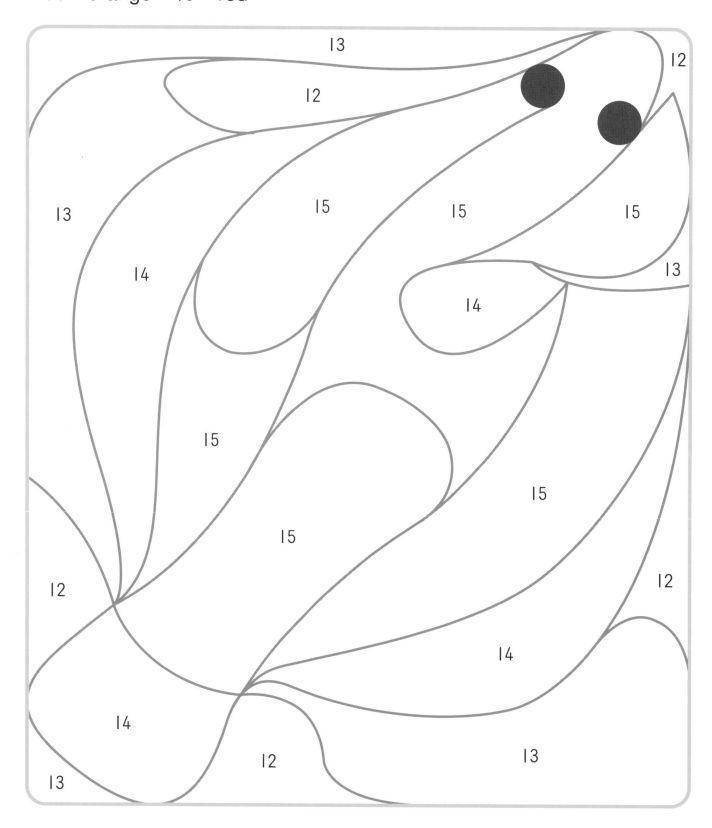

Happy Holidays!

Name

Date

■ Draw a line from 1 to 20 in order while saying each number.

What is it?

■ Use the key below to color by number.
16 = blue   17 = red

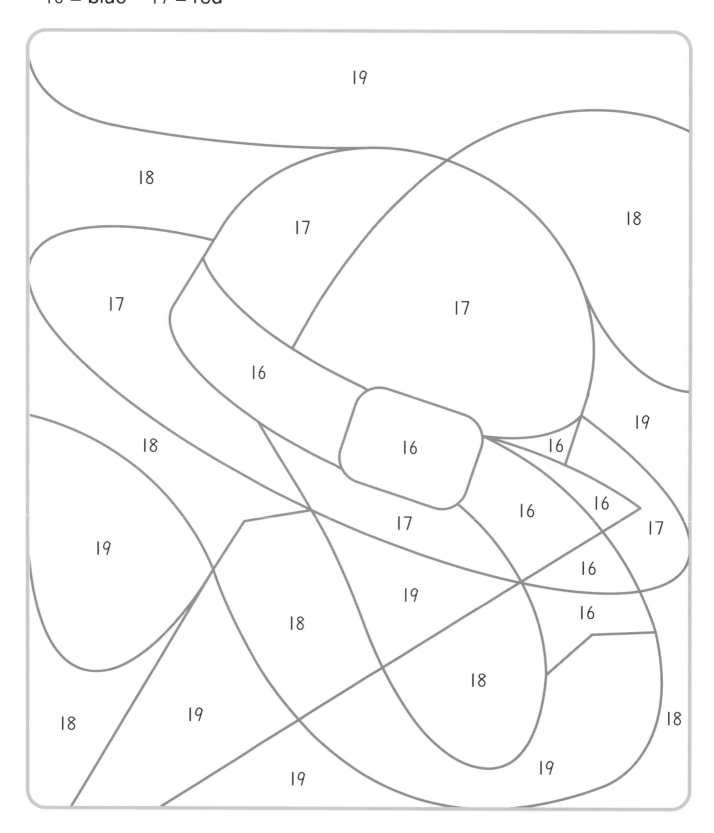

8 Rainy Days

Name

Date

■ Draw a line from I to 20 in order while saying each number.

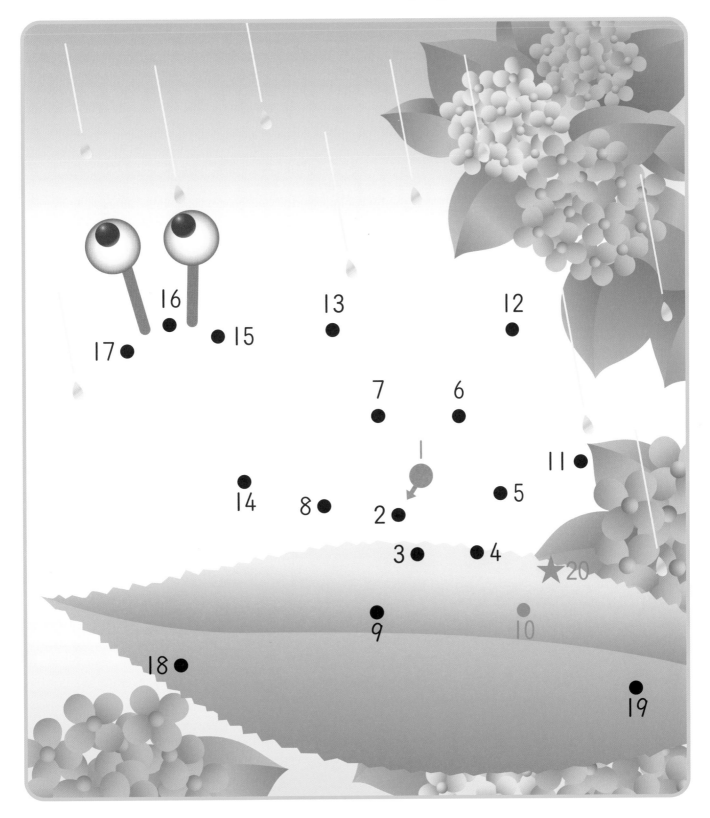

What is it?

■ Use the key below to color by number.
18 = brown   19 = yellow

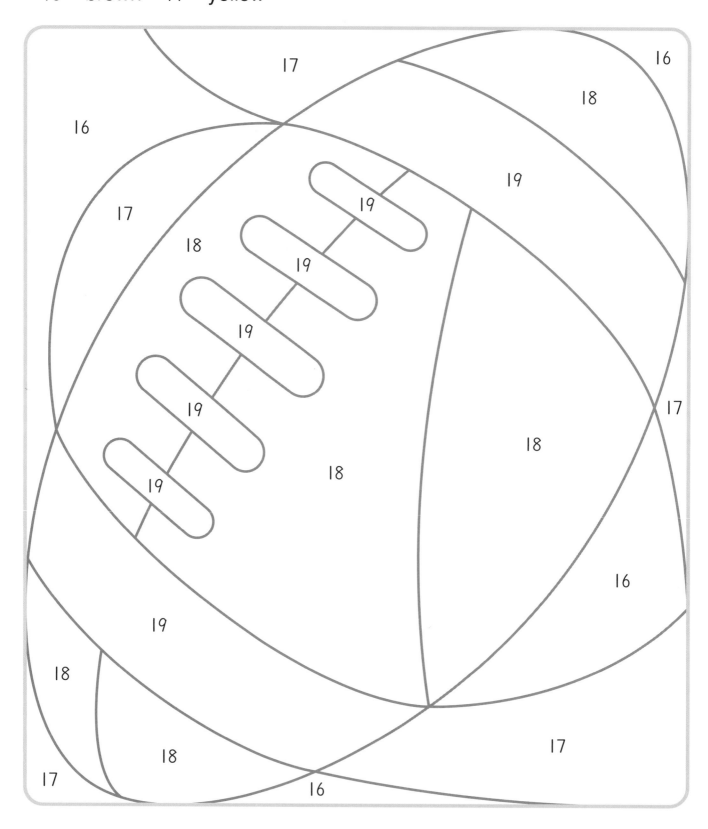

Lovely Flowers

Name

Date

To parents Starting on page 19, there are several points where children must draw a line that will cross another line. If your child has difficulty finding the numbers, please point them out for him or her. Please praise your child as he or she finishes each activity.

■ Draw a line from l to 20 in order while saying each number.

What is it?

■ Use the key below to color by number.
19 = green   20 = brown

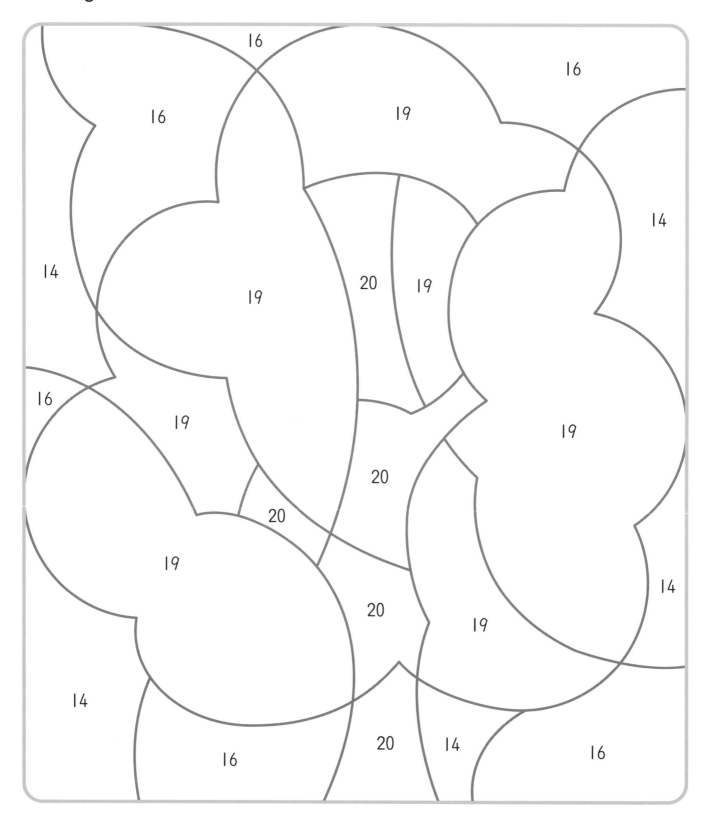

In the Forest

■ Draw a line from 1 to 30 in order while saying each number.

What is it?

■ Use the key below to color by number.
  21 = yellow   22 = green

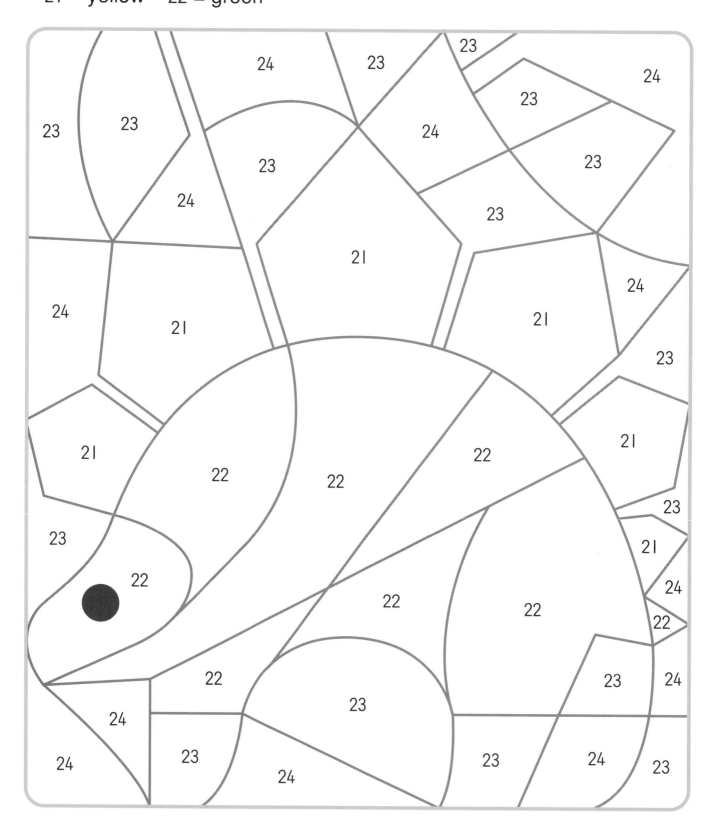

22

11 Is it a Beautiful Flower?

■ Draw a line from 1 to 30 in order while saying each number.

What is it?

■ Use the key below to color by number.
  23 = yellow   24 = black

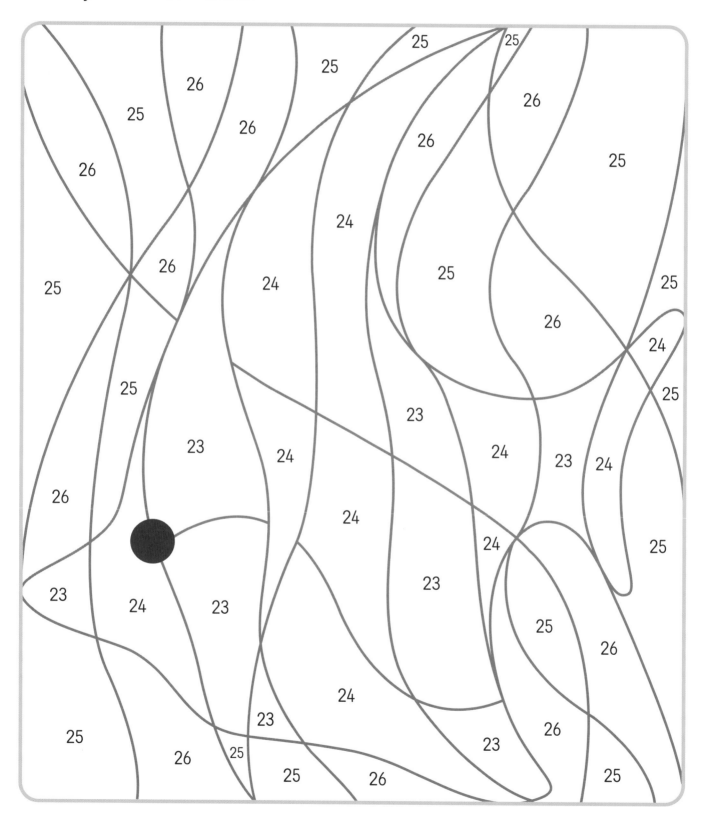

Who is Playing with the Ball?

■ Draw a line from 1 to 30 in order while saying each number.

What is it?

■ Use the key below to color by number.
26 = yellow   27 = blue

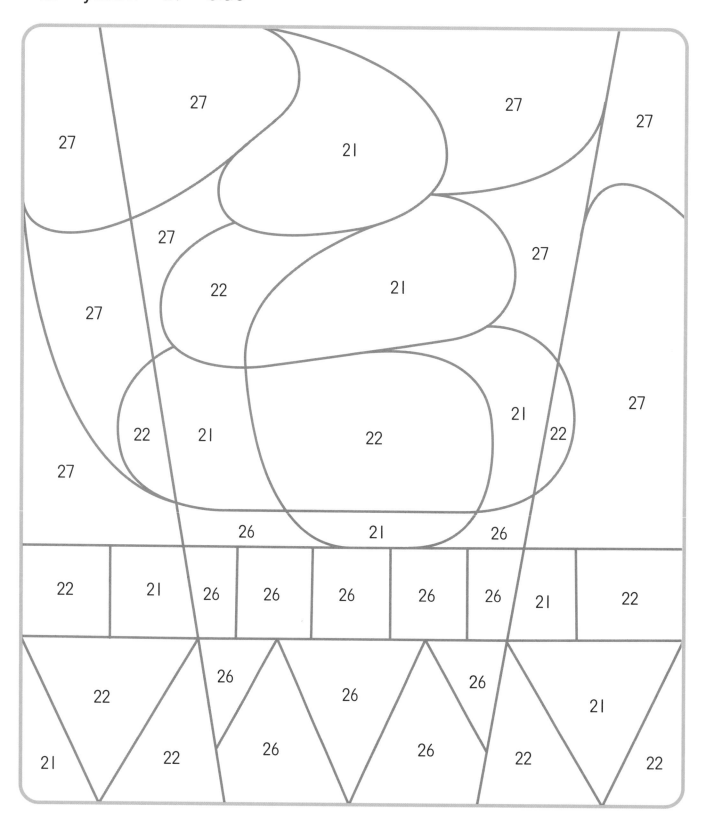

Look Out, Fly!

■ Draw a line from I to 30 in order while saying each number.

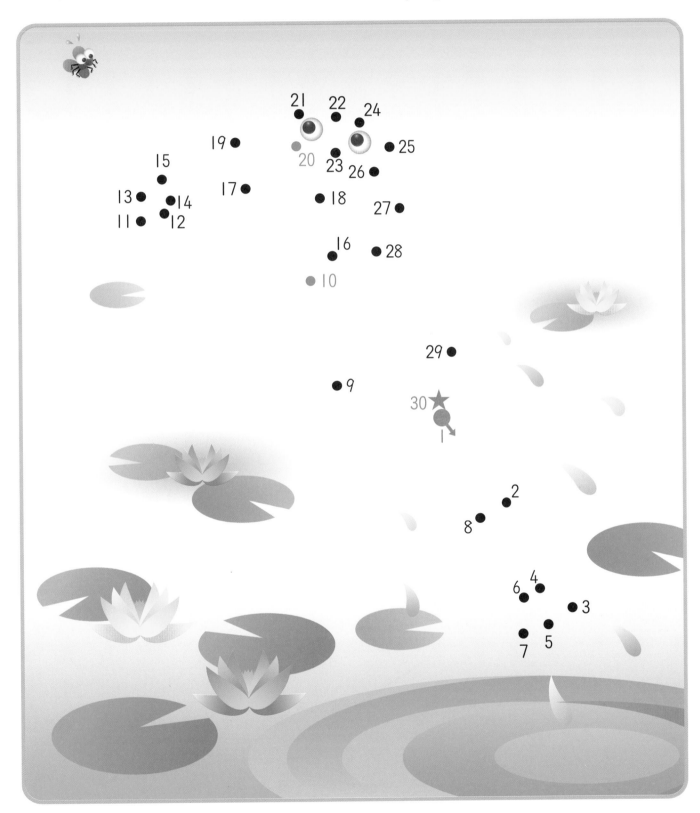

What is it?

■ Use the key below to color by number.
28 = brown   29 = blue   30 = green

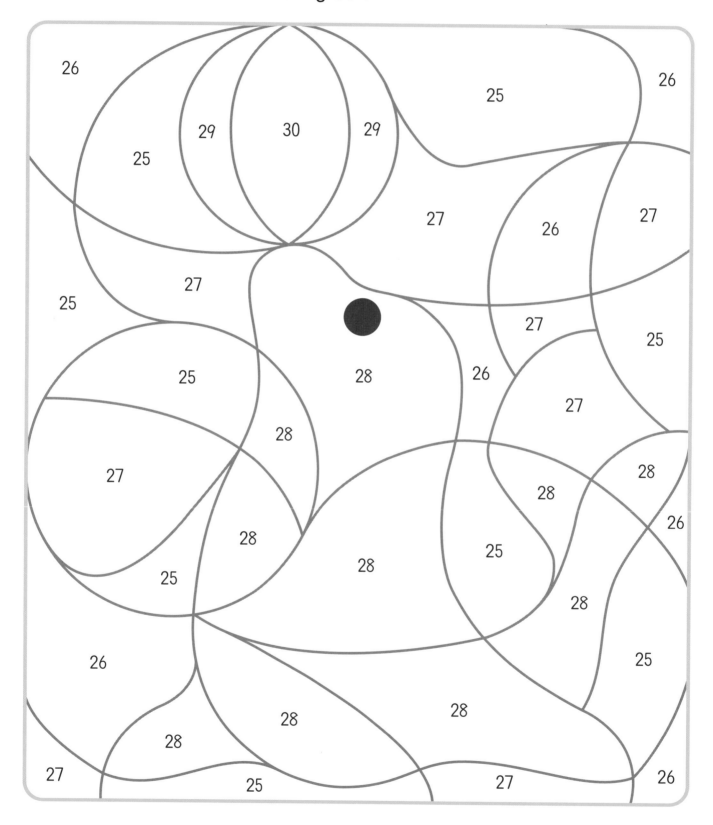

Gorilla Music

Name

Date

■ Draw a line from 1 to 30 in order while saying each number.

29

What is it?

■ Use the key below to color by number.
21 = blue   22 = green   23 = yellow

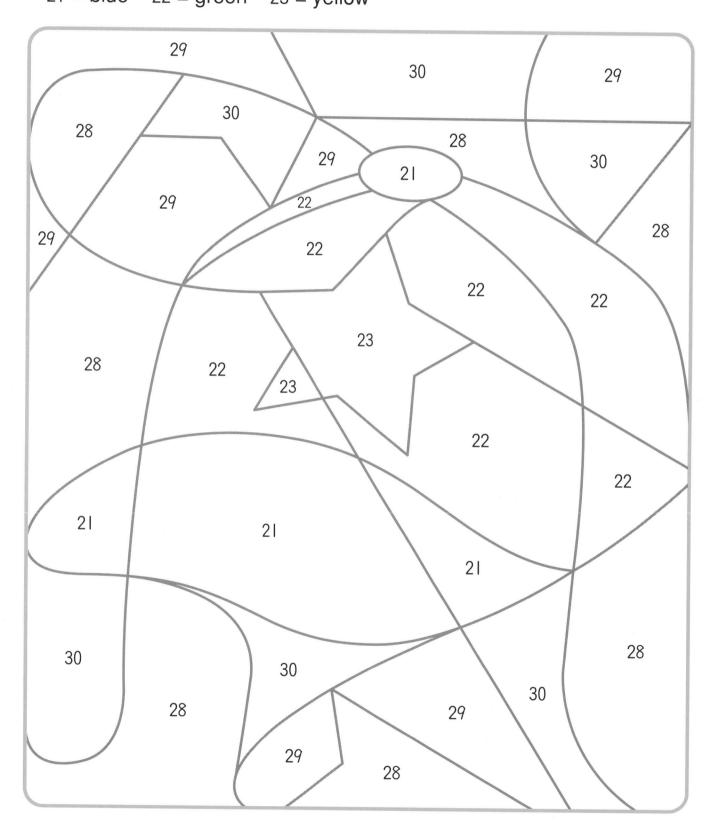

15 Up, Up, and Away!

Name

Date

■ Draw a line from 1 to 30 in order while saying each number.

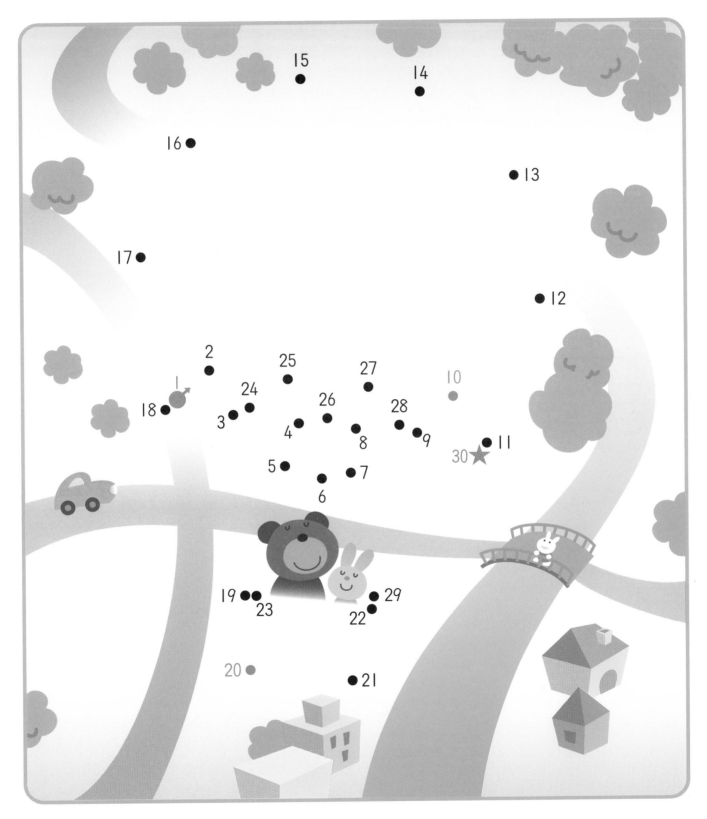

What is it?

■ Use the key below to color by number.
25 = blue   26 = orange   27 = yellow

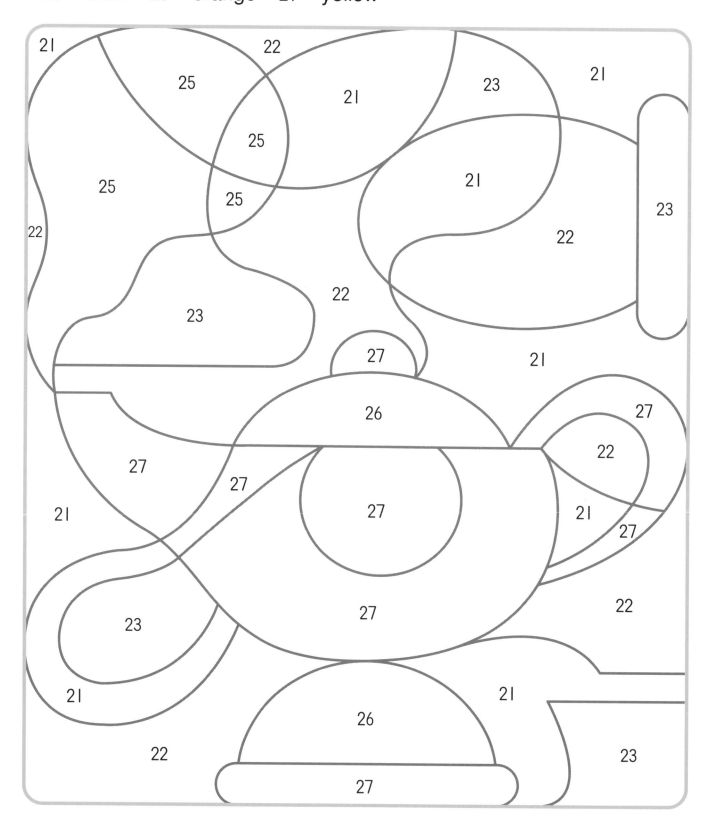

■ Draw a line from 1 to 40 in order while saying each number.

What is it?

■ Use the key below to color by number.
31 = red   32 = orange   33 = green

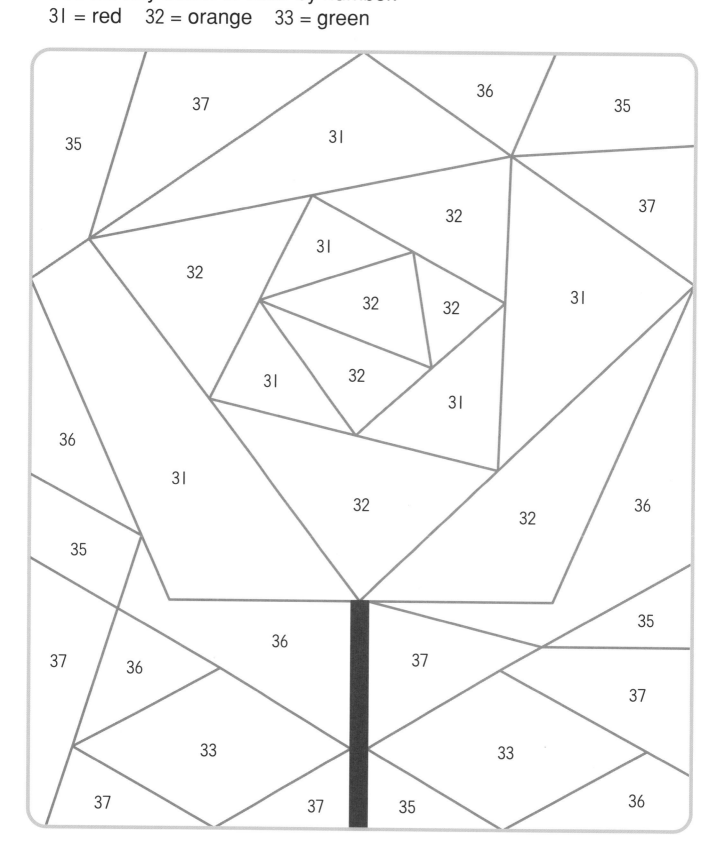

17 Nice to See You Again

Name

Date

■ Draw a line from 1 to 40 in order while saying each number.

What is it?

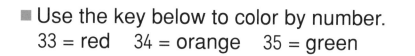

■ Use the key below to color by number.
  33 = red   34 = orange   35 = green

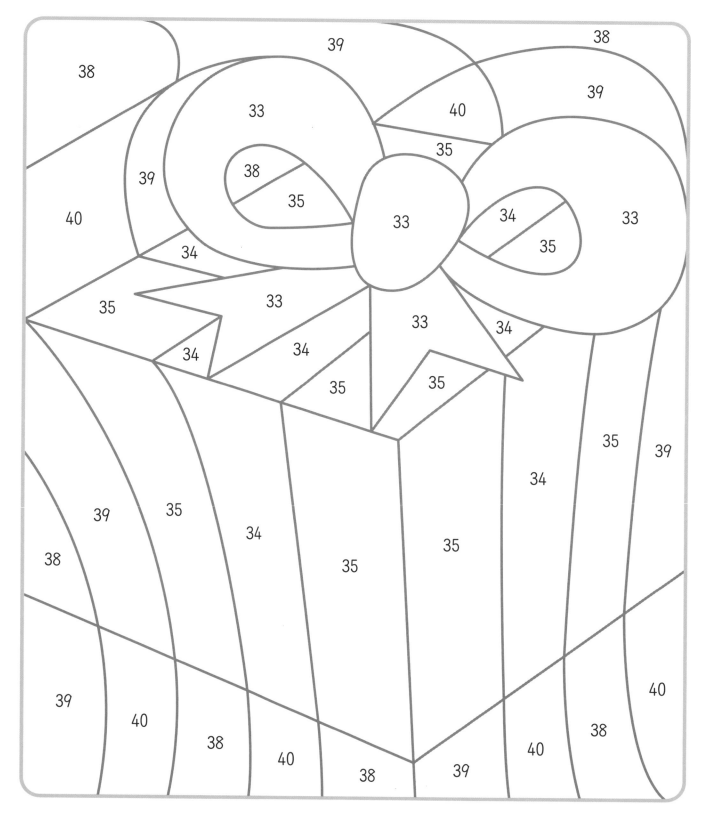

18 Moonlight Music

Name

Date

■ Draw a line from 1 to 40 in order while saying each number.

What is it?

■ Use the key below to color by number.
  36 = red   37 = yellow   38 = orange

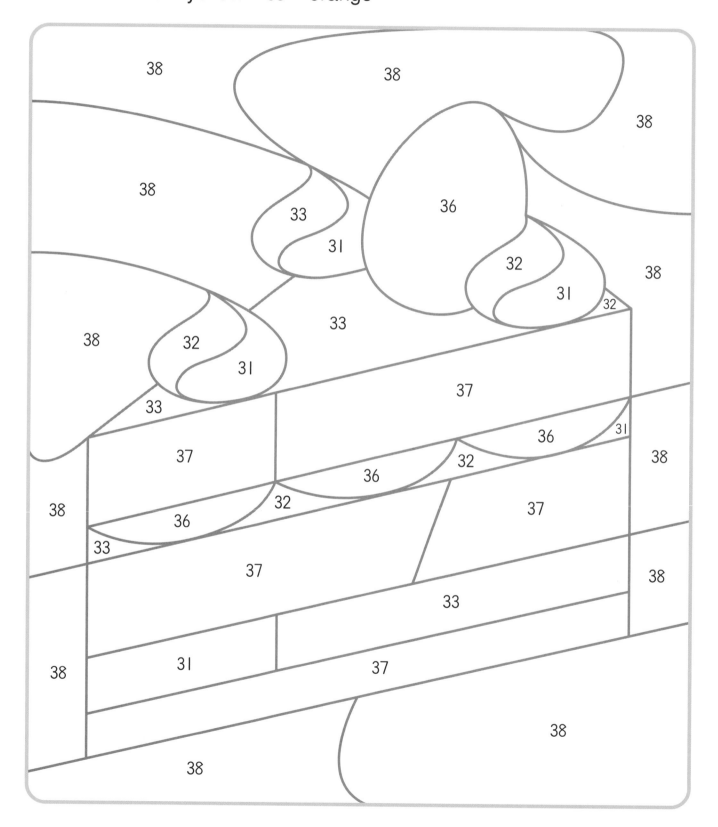

Who Eats these Leaves?

■ Draw a line from 1 to 40 in order while saying each number.

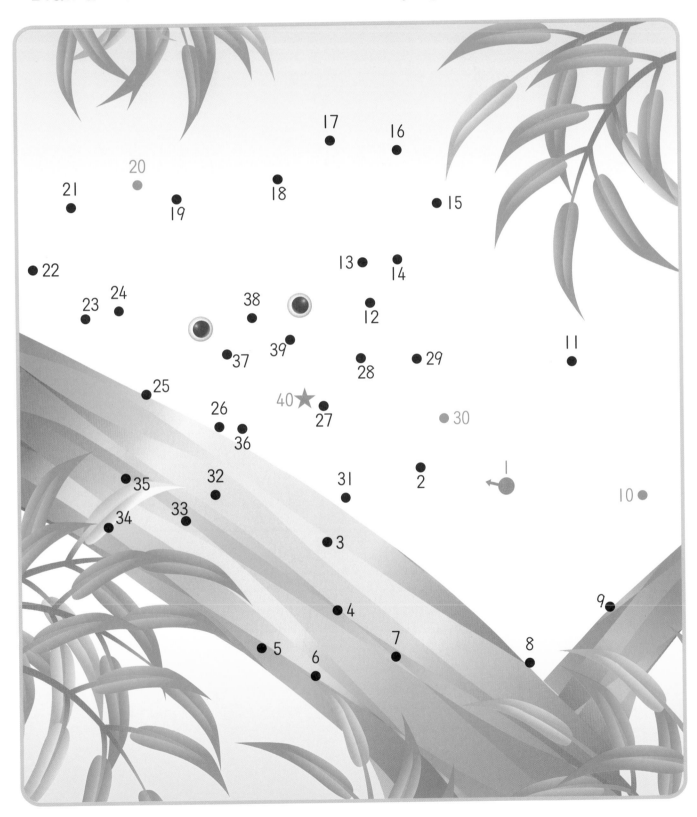

What is it?

■ Use the key below to color by number.
38 = yellow   39 = green   40 = red

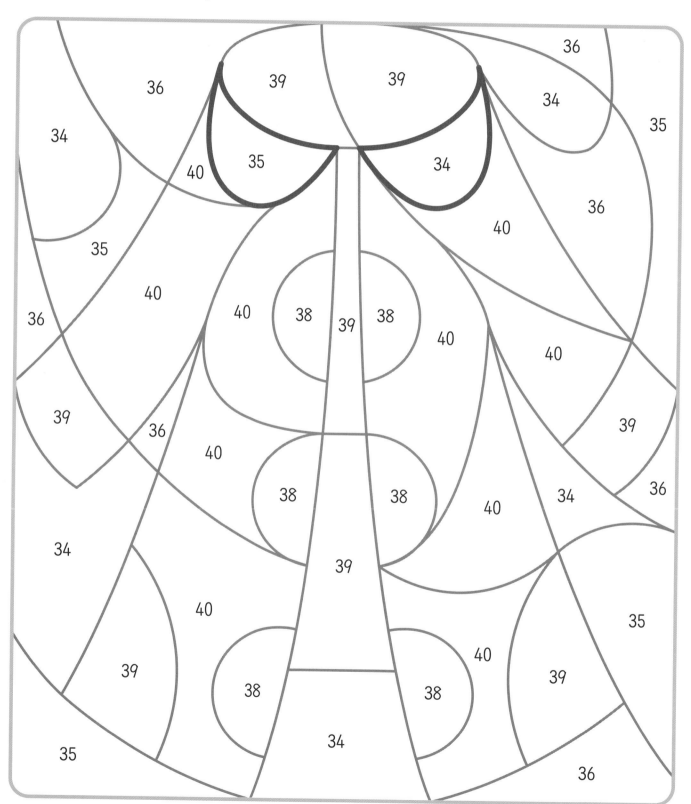

40

 **What a Catch!**

Name

Date

■ Draw a line from 1 to 40 in order while saying each number.

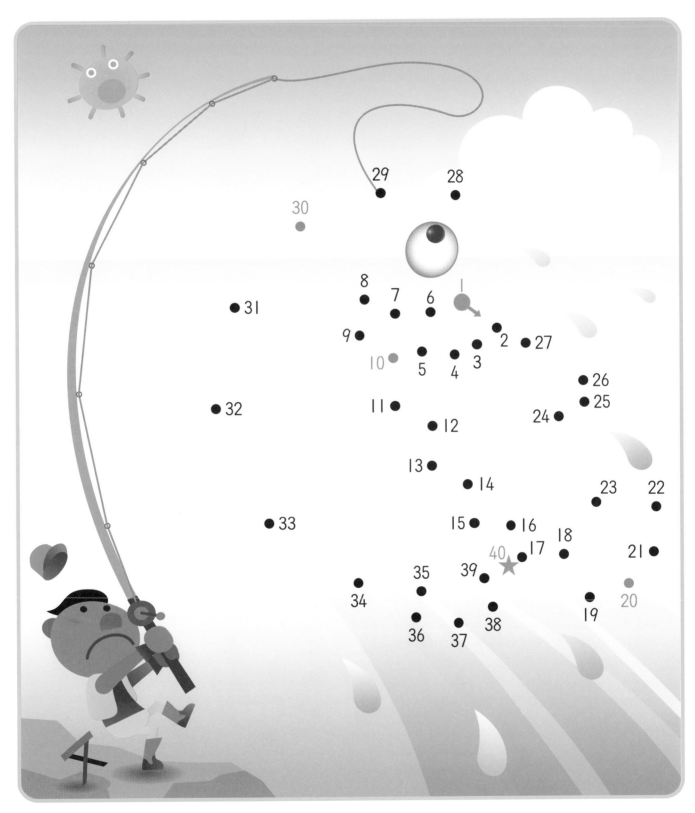

41

What is it?

■ Use the key below to color by number.
   31 = black   34 = orange   36 = yellow

21 At the Circus

■ Draw a line from 1 to 40 in order while saying each number.

43

What is it?

Use the key below to color by number.

32 = orange   35 = red   39 = yellow   40 = blue

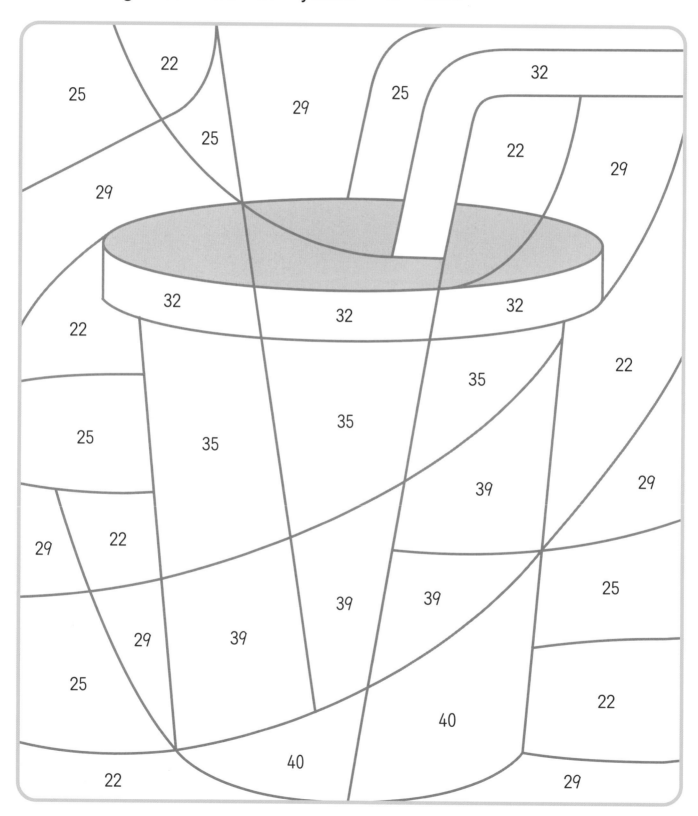

44

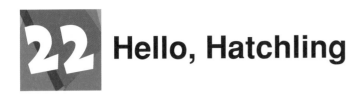

22 Hello, Hatchling

Name

Date

■ Draw a line from 1 to 40 in order while saying each number.

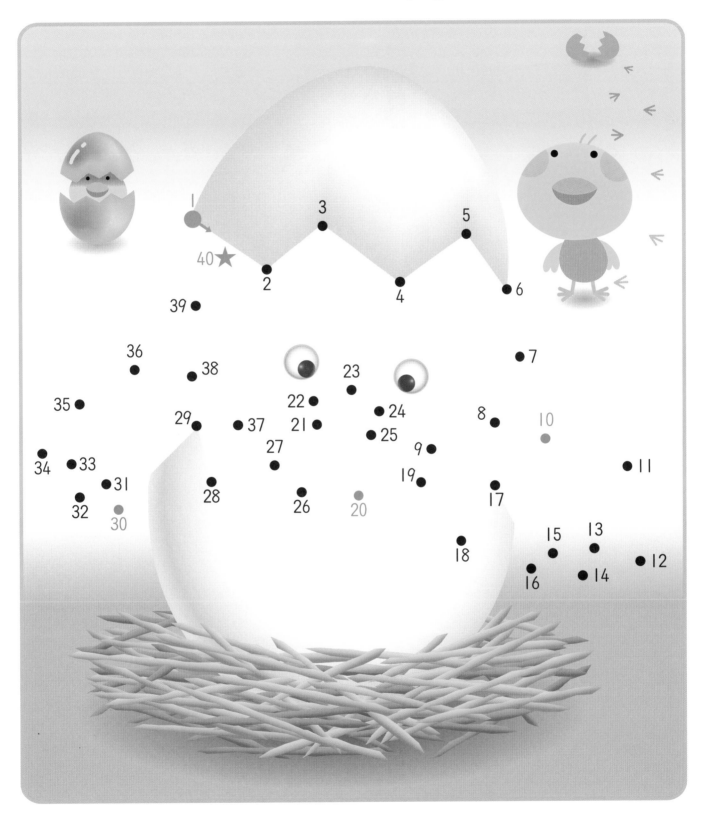

What is it?

■ Use the key below to color by number.
33 = yellow   37 = red   38 = violet (purple)   40 = brown

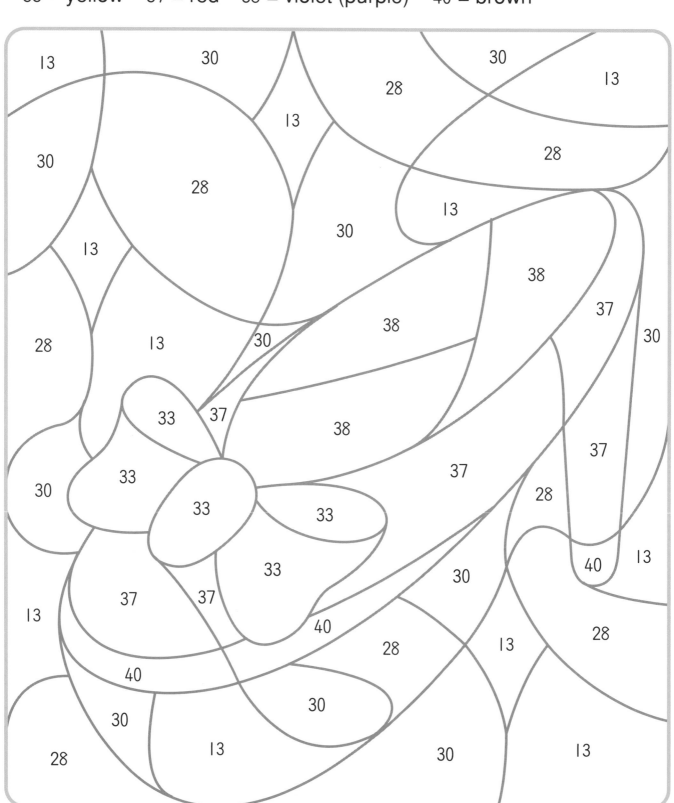

23 Who's in the Egg?

■ Draw a line from 1 to 50 in order while saying each number.

47

What is it?

Use the key below to color by number.
41 = yellow   42 = blue   43 = black   44 = green

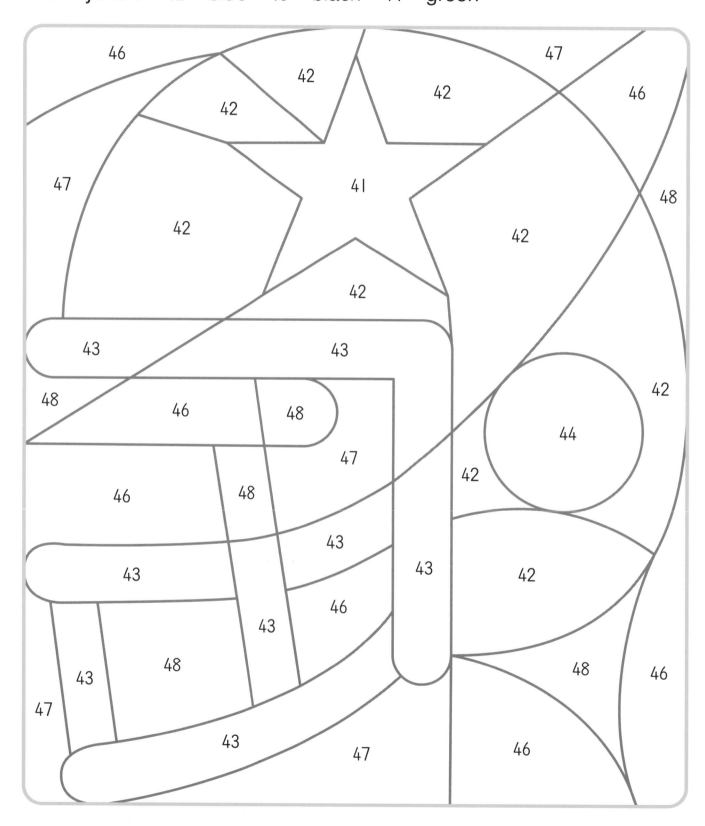

24 In Mommy's Pocket

Name

Date

■ Draw a line from 1 to 50 in order while saying each number.

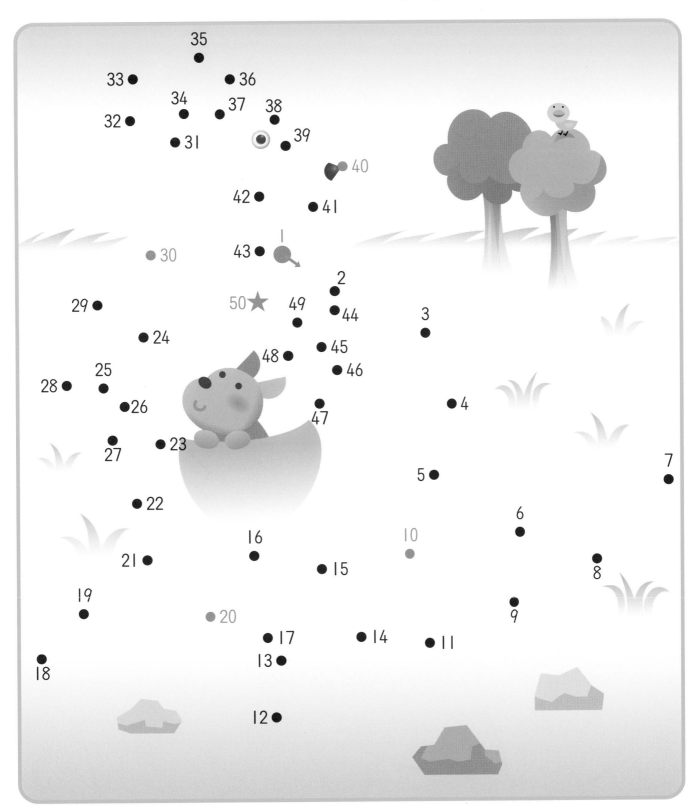

What is it?

■ Use the key below to color by number.
45 = orange   46 = yellow   47 = blue   48 = violet (purple)

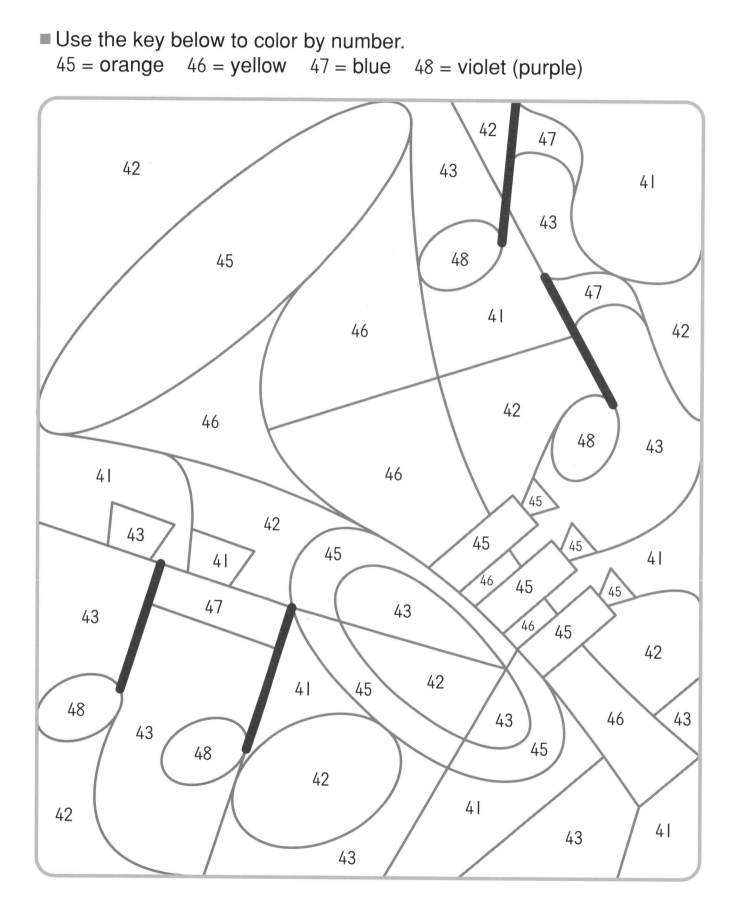

Name

Date

■ Draw a line from 1 to 50 in order while saying each number.

What is it?

■ Use the key below to color by number.
   47 = violet (purple)   48 = yellow   49 = orange   50 = red

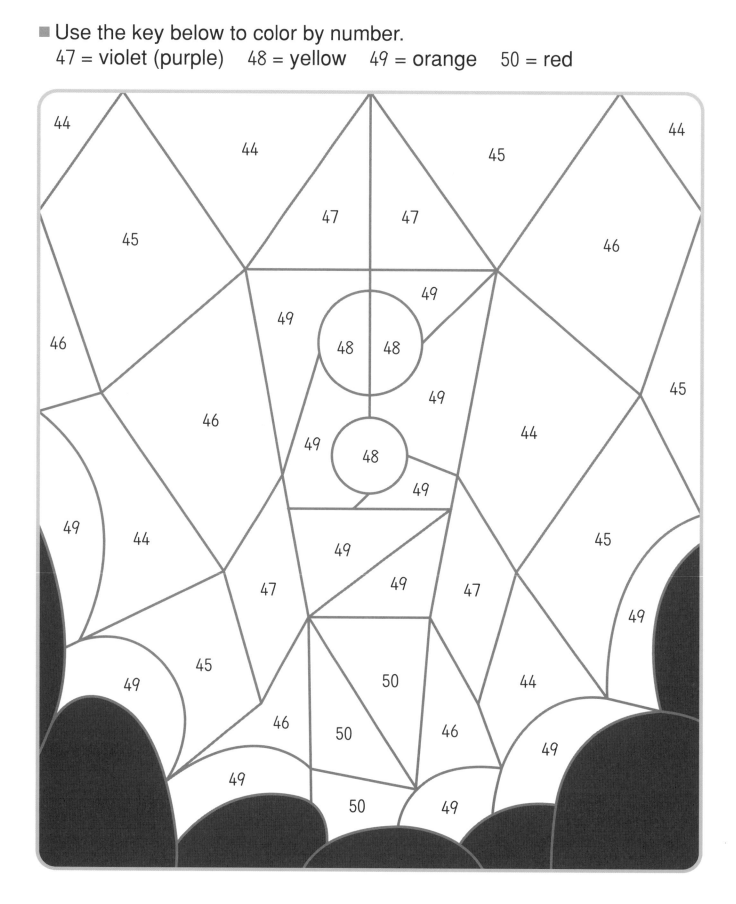

26 A Light under the Sea

Name

Date

■ Draw a line from 1 to 50 in order while saying each number.

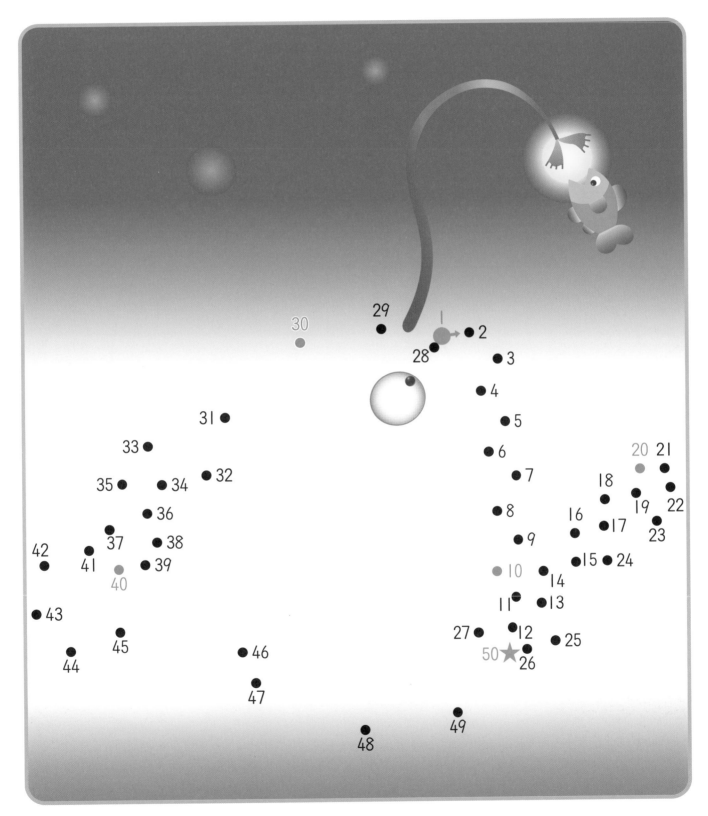

What is it?

■ Use the key below to color by number.
41 = blue   43 = black   44 = green   47 = yellow

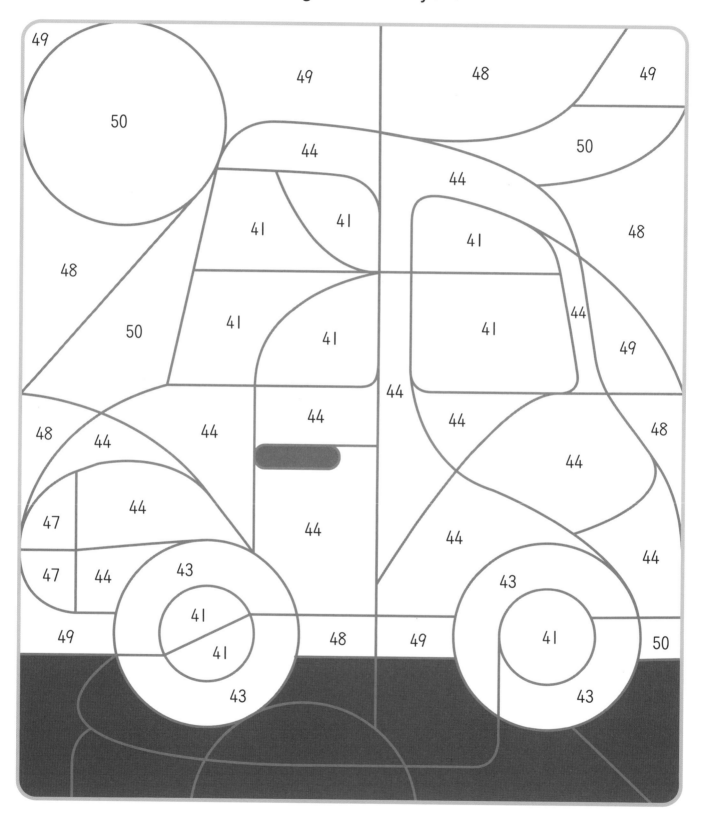

54

■ Draw a line from 1 to 50 in order while saying each number.

What is it?

■ Use the key below to color by number.
42 = brown   45 = blue   46 = green   49 = yellow   50 = violet (purple)

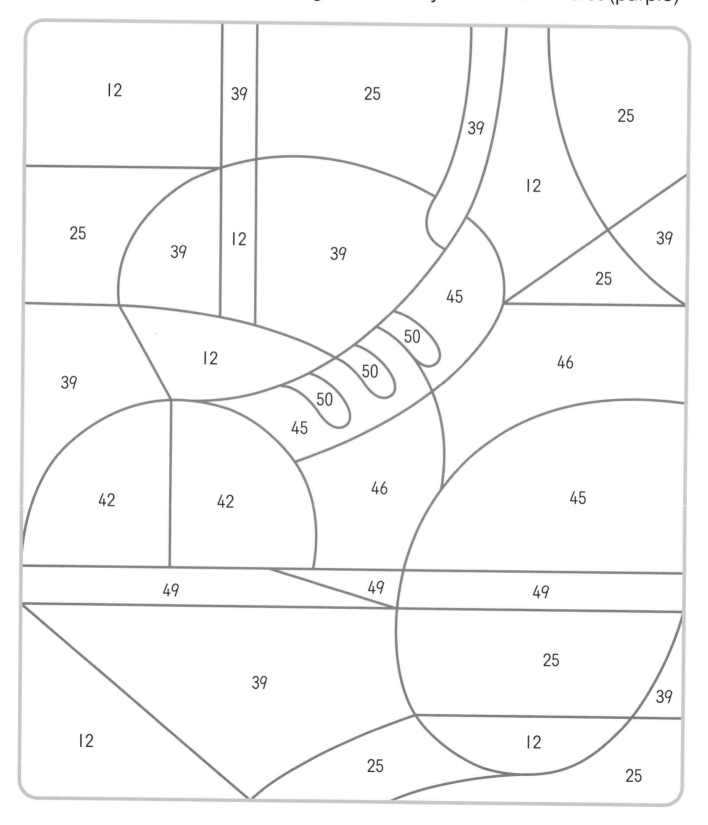

56

28 Have You Found Me?

Name

Date

To parents On this page, your child will have to draw many lines that cross other lines. If your child has difficulty finding the numbers, please point them out for him or her. Please praise your child as he or she finishes each activity.

■ Draw a line from 1 to 50 in order while saying each number.

What is it?

Use the key below to color by number.
41 = black   43 = blue   44 = yellow   47 = green   48 = violet (purple)

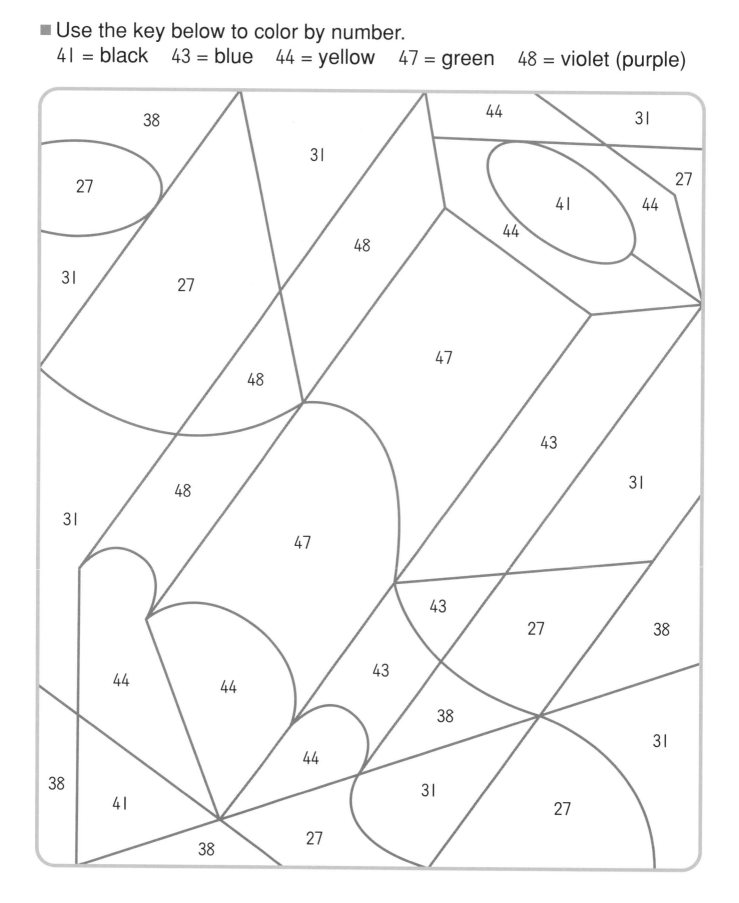

Name

Date

■ Draw a line from 1 to 50 in order while saying each number.

What is it?

■ Use the key below to color by number.

42 = red   43 = blue   45 = black   49 = violet (purple)   50 = orange

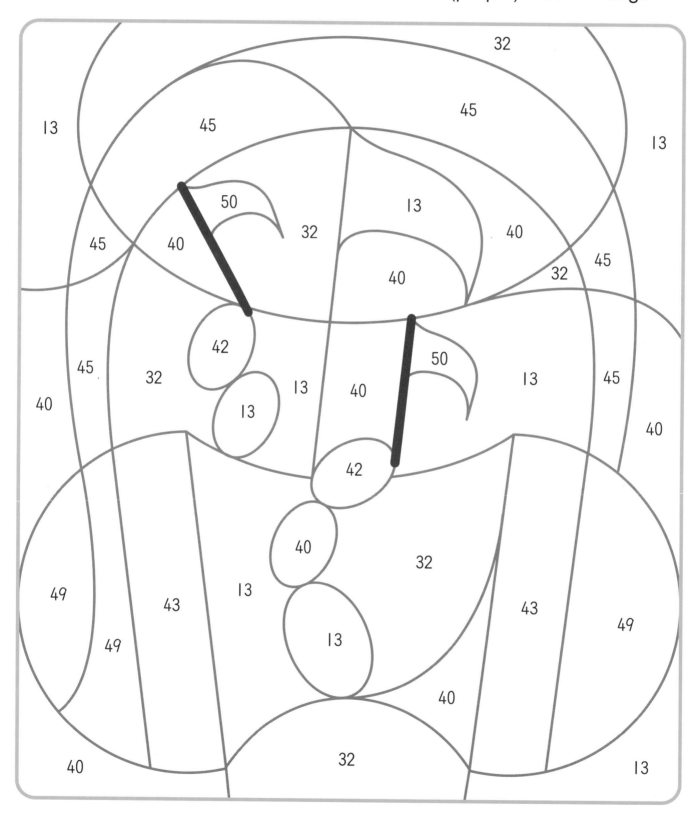

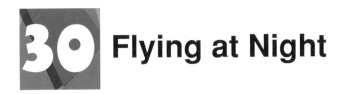

30 Flying at Night

Name

Date

■ Draw a line from 1 to 50 in order while saying each number.

What is it?

■ Use the key below to color by number.
41 = blue   42 = yellow   44 = violet (purple)   46 = brown   48 = green

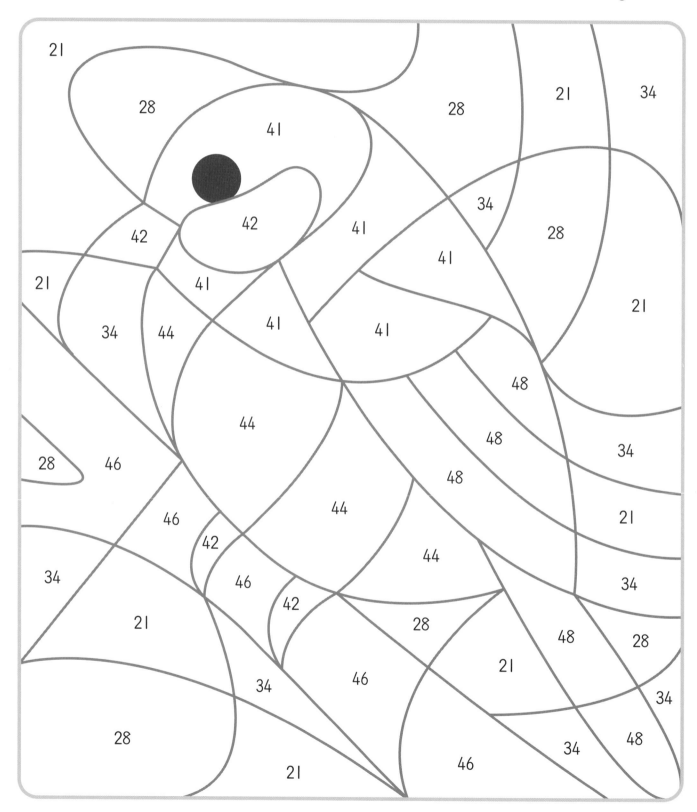

31 Look Out, Mouse!

■ Draw a line from 1 to 50 in order while saying each number.

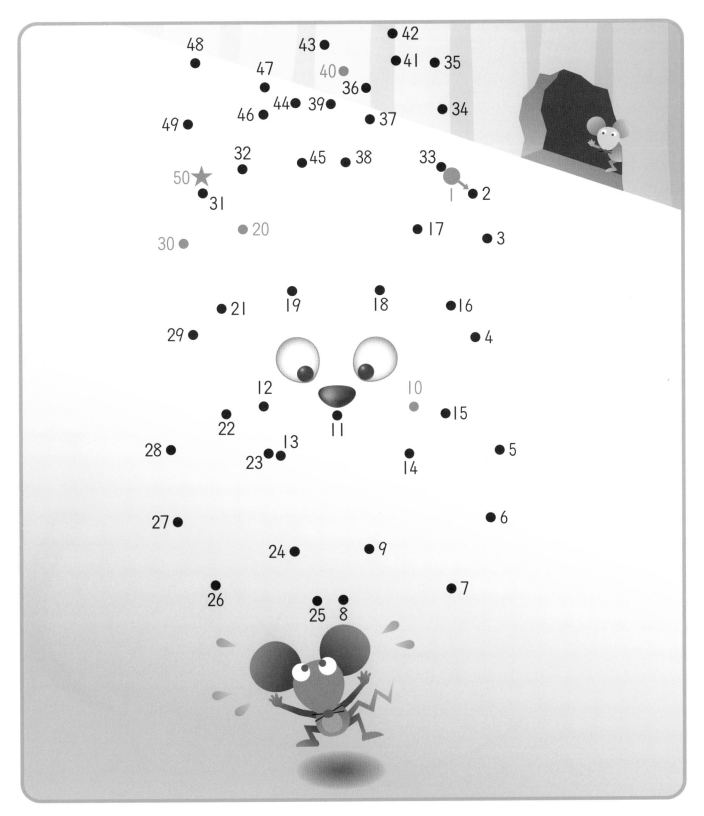

63

What is it?

■ Use the key below to color by number.

43 = orange   45 = brown   47 = yellow   49 = red   50 = black

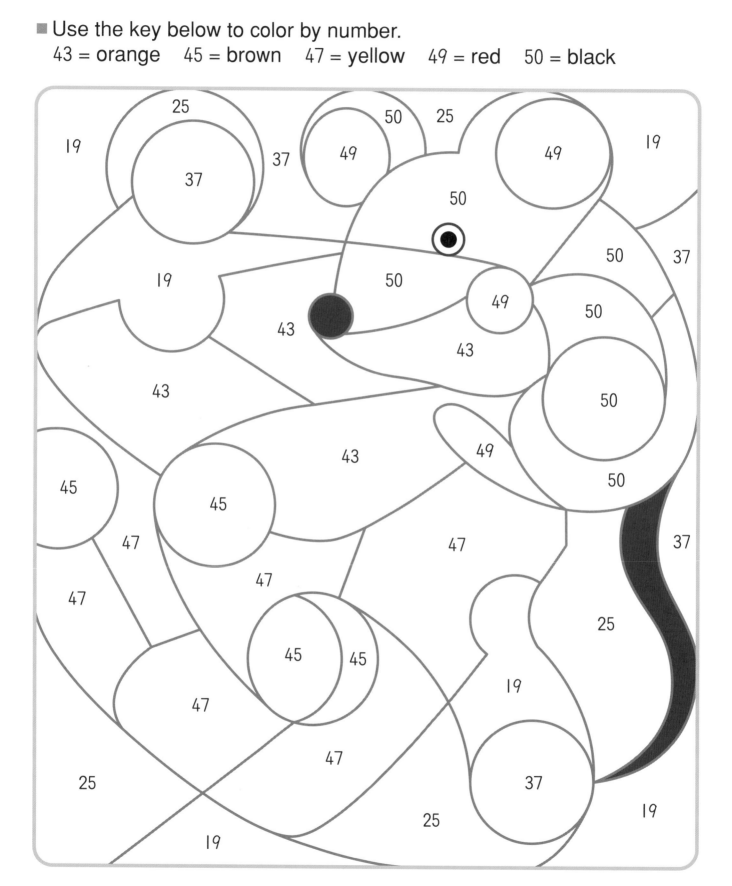

64

32 Ice Skating

Name

Date

■ Draw a line from 1 to 60 in order while saying each number.

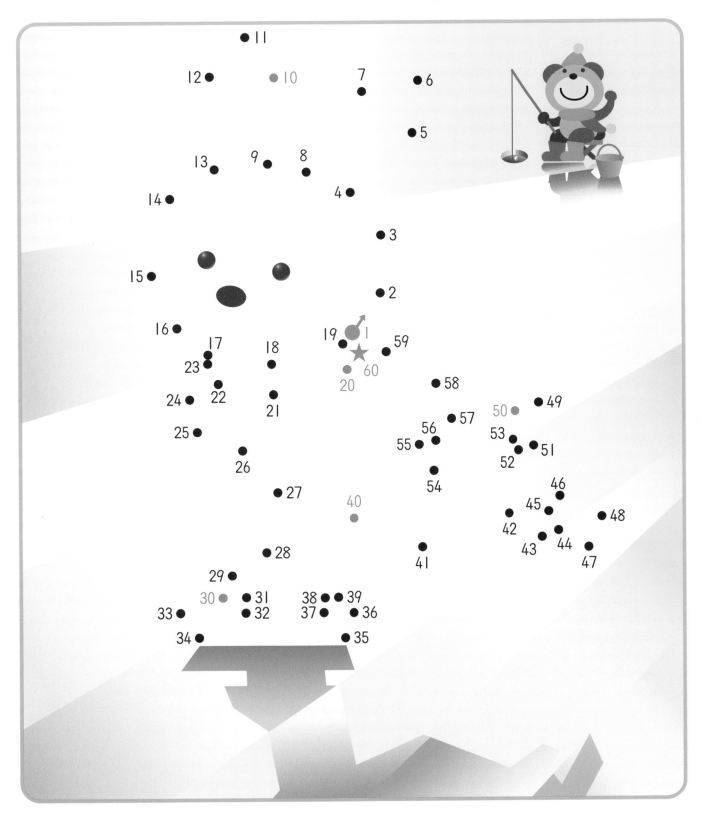

65

What is it?

■ Use the key below to color by number.
51 = black   52 = brown   53 = green   54 = red   55 = yellow

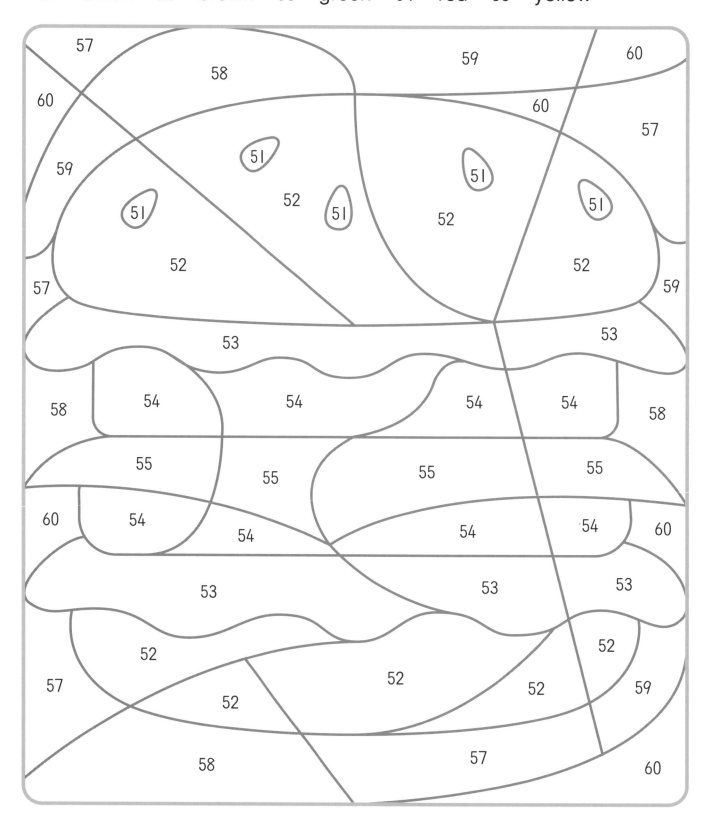

33 Can You Spot Me?

Name

Date

To parents Starting on page 67, the numbers become more difficult to find. If your child has difficulty finding the numbers, please point them out for him or her. Please praise your child as he or she finishes each activity.

■ Draw a line from 1 to 60 in order while saying each number.

What is it?

■ Use the key below to color by number.

56 = green   57 = blue   58 = black   59 = yellow   60 = violet (purple)

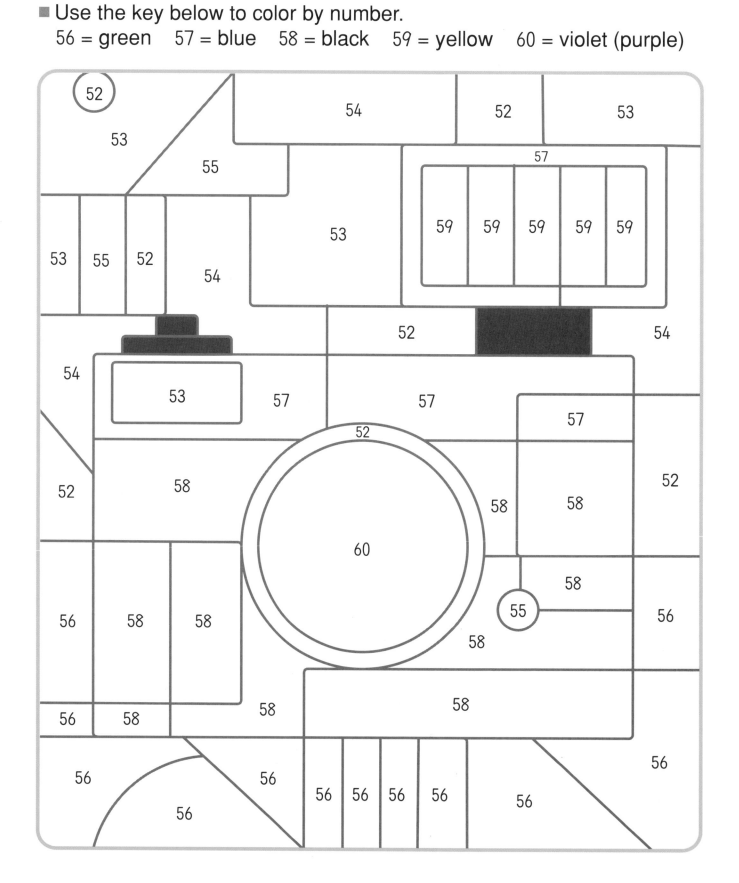

Name

Date

■ Draw a line from 1 to 60 in order while saying each number.

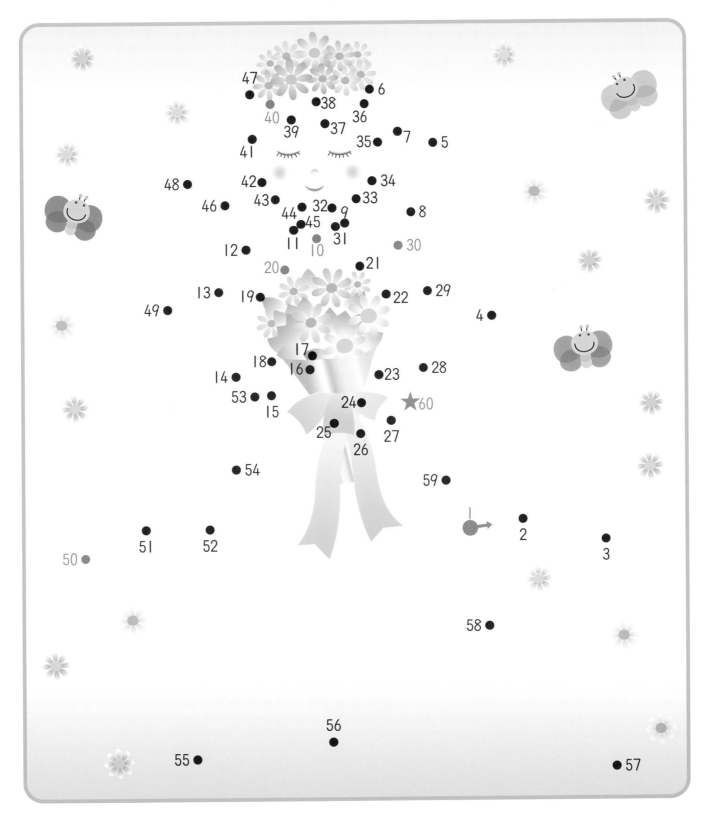

69

What is it?

■ Use the key below to color by number.

52 = black 53 = orange 54 = yellow 55 = blue 58 = red 59 = green

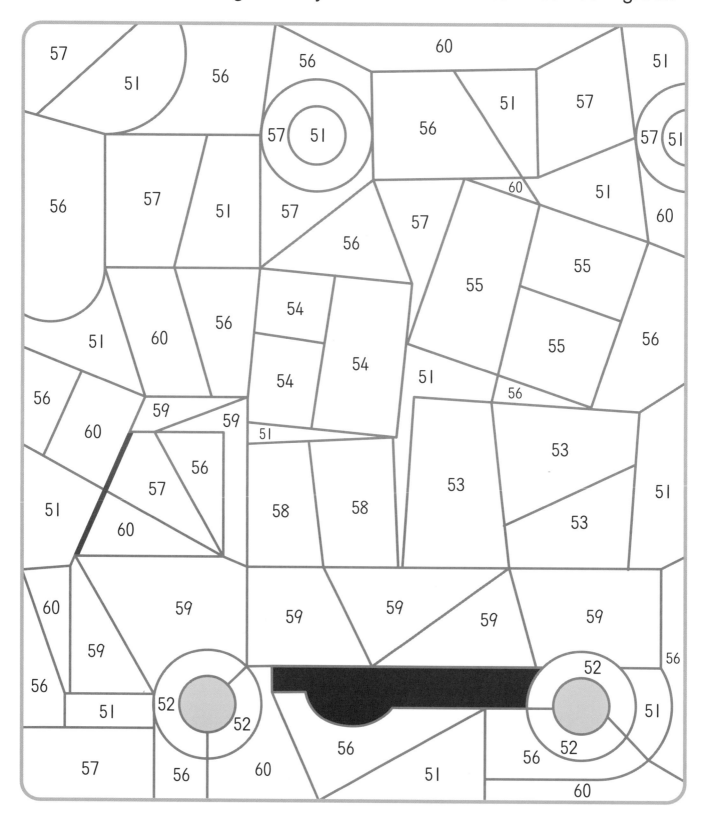

70

Eek! A Bug!

■ Draw a line from 1 to 70 in order while saying each number.

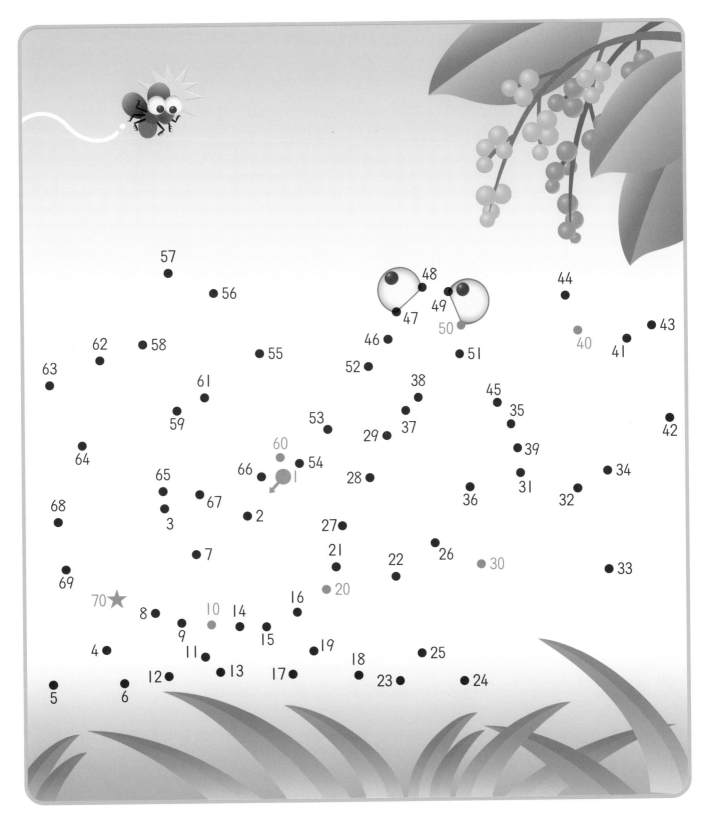

What is it?

■ Use the key below to color by number.
  61 = yellow 62 = red 63 = blue 64 = green 65 = orange 66 = brown

72

Help Me!

Name

Date

■ Draw a line from 1 to 70 in order while saying each number.

What is it?

■ Use the key below to color by number.
   65 = red   66 = yellow   67 = blue   68 = green   69 = orange   70 = black

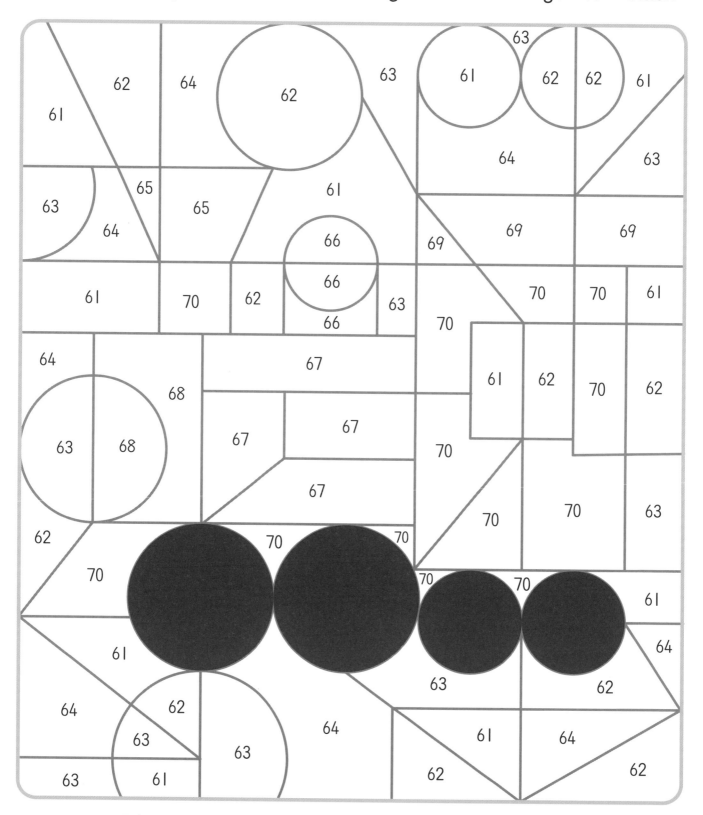

Oops!

Draw a line from 1 to 70 in order while saying each number.

What is it?

■ Use the key below to color by number.
62 = blue   63 = red   64 = yellow   65 = black   66 = orange   68 = brown

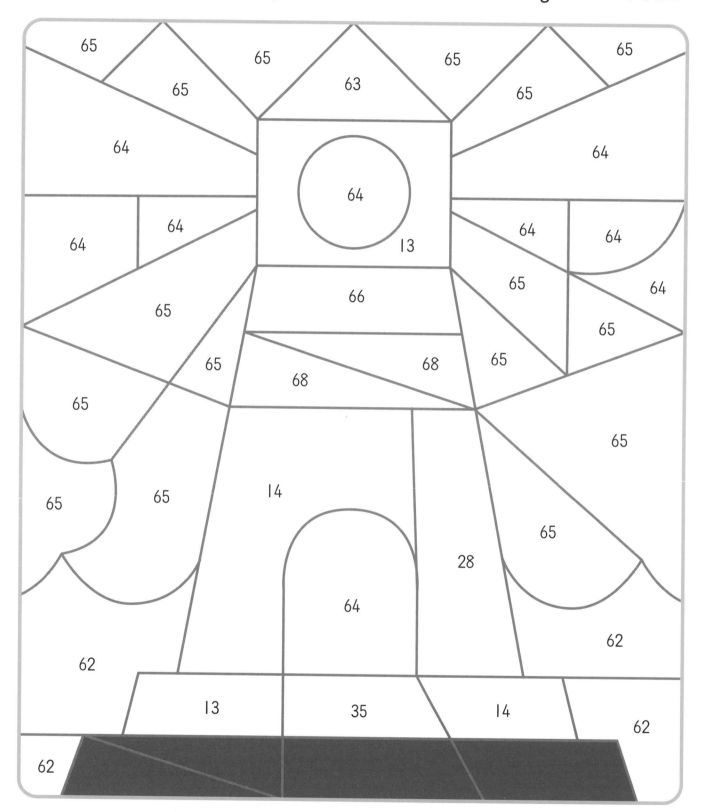

Who is Juggling?

Name

Date

■ Draw a line from 1 to 70 in order while saying each number.

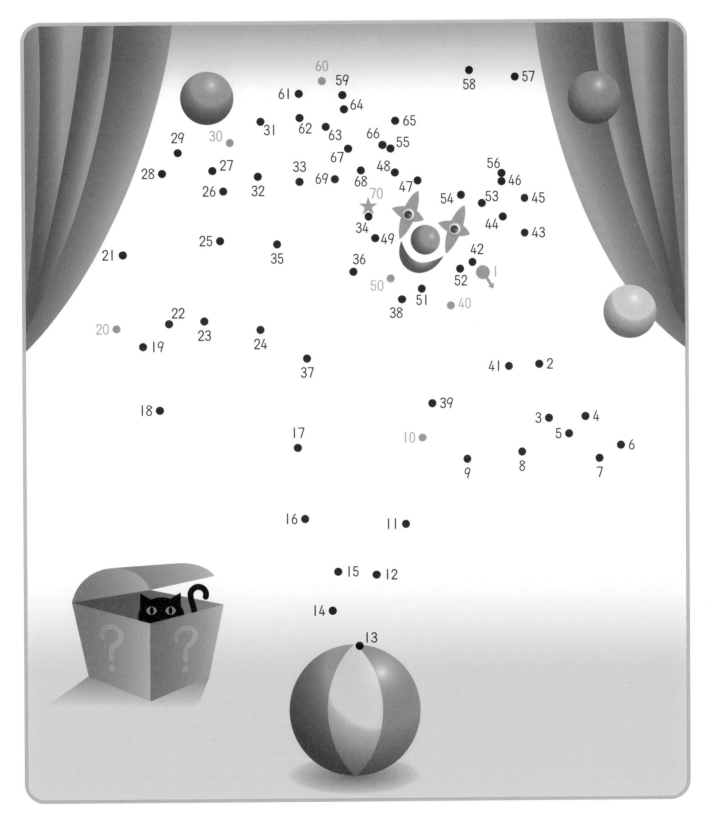

What is it?

To parents This is the last page of this section. Your child has been developing number recognition and number sequence skills. Please offer your child lots of praise for completing the section.

■ Use the key below to color by number.

61 = yellow   64 = orange   67 = red   68 = violet (purple)   69 = black   70 = blue

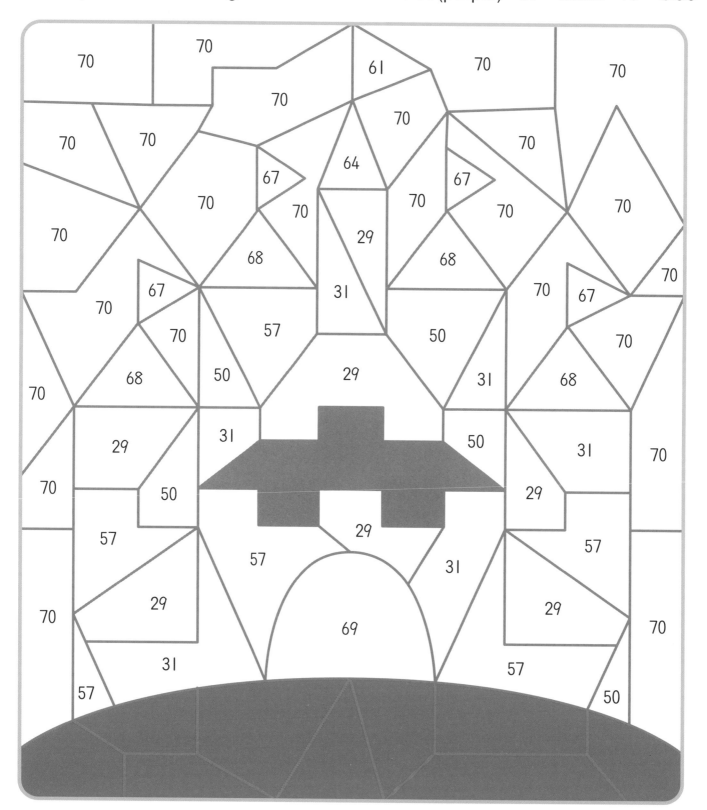

Answer Key

p. 3 cake

p. 4 star

p. 5 doghouse

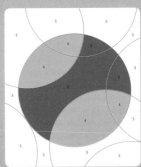

p. 6 ball

p. 7 hang glider

p. 8 green pepper

p. 9 lightning

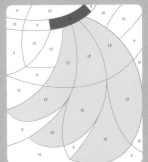

p. 10 bunch of bananas

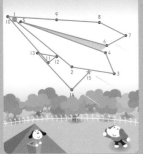

p. 11 paper airplane

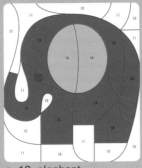

p. 12 elephant

p. 13 tent

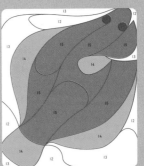

p. 14 flounder

p. 15 holiday tree

p. 16 hat

p. 17 snail

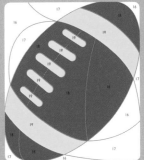

p. 18 football

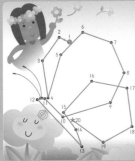

p. 19 butterfly

p. 20 tree

p. 21 snake

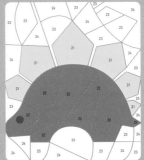

p. 22 Stegosaurus

79

Answer Key

p. 23 mole

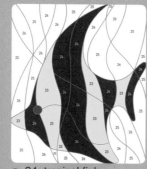

p. 24 tropical fish

p. 25 sea lion

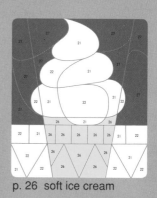

p. 26 soft ice cream

p. 27 frog

p. 28 seal

p. 29 piano

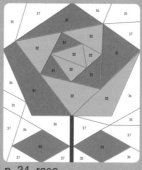

p. 30 cap

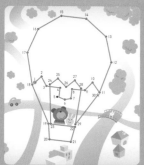

p. 31 balloon

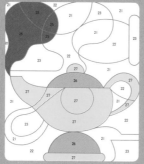

p. 32 magic lamp

p. 33 whale

p. 34 rose

p. 35 pig

p. 36 present

p. 37 wolf

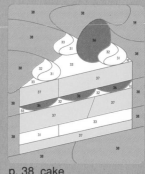

p. 38 cake

p. 39 koala

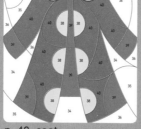

p. 40 coat

p. 41 puffer fish

p. 42 cat

Answer Key

p. 43 elephant

p. 44 drink

p. 45 hatching chick

p. 46 high-heeled shoe

p. 47 hatching Tyrannosaurus

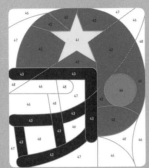

p. 48 helmet

p. 49 kangaroo

p. 50 trumpet

p. 51 flatfish

p. 52 rocket

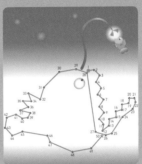

p. 53 angler fish

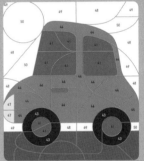

p. 54 car

p. 55 grasshopper

p. 56 sneaker

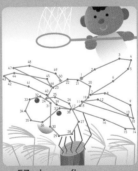

p. 57 dragonfly

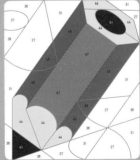

p. 58 pencil

p. 59 horse

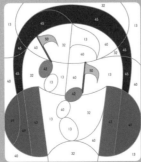

p. 60 headphones

p. 61 bat

p. 62 bird

Answer Key

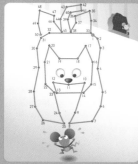

p. 63 cat

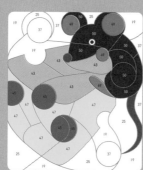

p. 64 mouse and cheese

p. 65 rabbit

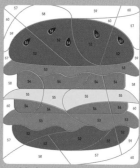

p. 66 hamburger

p. 67 leopard

p. 68 camera

p. 69 bride

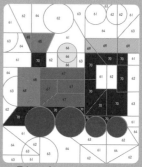

p. 70 truck

p. 71 praying mantis

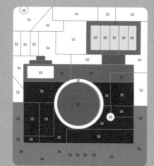

p. 72 holiday tree

p. 73 bear

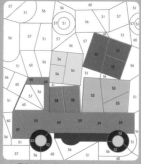

p. 74 train

p. 75 dog

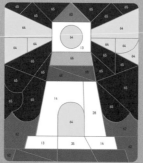

p. 76 lighthouse

p. 77 clown

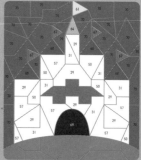

p. 78 castle

82

My Big Book of NUMBERS, LETTERS & WORDS

ALPHABET GAMES

Table of Contents

To parents: ALPHABET GAMES

In this section, your child will have the opportunity to solidify his or her current understanding of the alphabet, by practicing uppercase and lowercase letters in order. Your child will strengthen his or her pencil control skills, while reinforcing the concept of alphabetical order. The tracing and dot-to-dot activities in this section also emphasize learning alphabetical order in a fun format.

Later in this section, your child will practice uppercase and lowercase letters in pairs, which will allow him or her to link the two letters in alphabetic pairs. Lastly, the characters and animals through this part illustrate the use of uppercase and lowercase letters for names and words. This section is designed so your child will learn the shapes and sounds of the letters of the alphabet.

The activities in this section will help your child build a foundation for future reading and writing skills. If your child is ready to advance to the next skill after completing this section, please refer to the appropriate book from our other Verbal Skills products for further work.

My Book of
WRITING WORDS

My Book of
SIMPLE SENTENCES

My Book of
SENTENCES

How to hold a pencil properly

There are several ways to teach children to hold a pencil properly.
Here is one example.

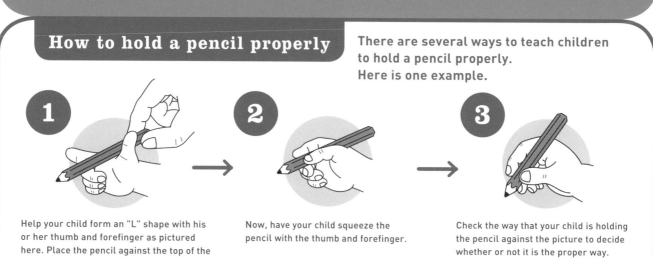

1 Help your child form an "L" shape with his or her thumb and forefinger as pictured here. Place the pencil against the top of the bent middle finger and on the thumb joint.

2 Now, have your child squeeze the pencil with the thumb and forefinger.

3 Check the way that your child is holding the pencil against the picture to decide whether or not it is the proper way.

It can be difficult for a child who does not yet have enough strength in his or her hand and fingers to hold the pencil properly. Please teach this skill gradually, so that your child will remaln interested and willing to hold a pencil naturally.

Uppercase Letters
Saying "A·B·C"

To parents
Guide your child to write his or her name and date in the box above. On this page, your child will connect the first three uppercase letters of the alphabet. From this page on, the number of letters will gradually increase. Please have your child say the letters aloud while he or she is tracing.

Name

Date

■ While saying each letter aloud, draw a line from "A" to "C" to connect the letters in alphabetical order.

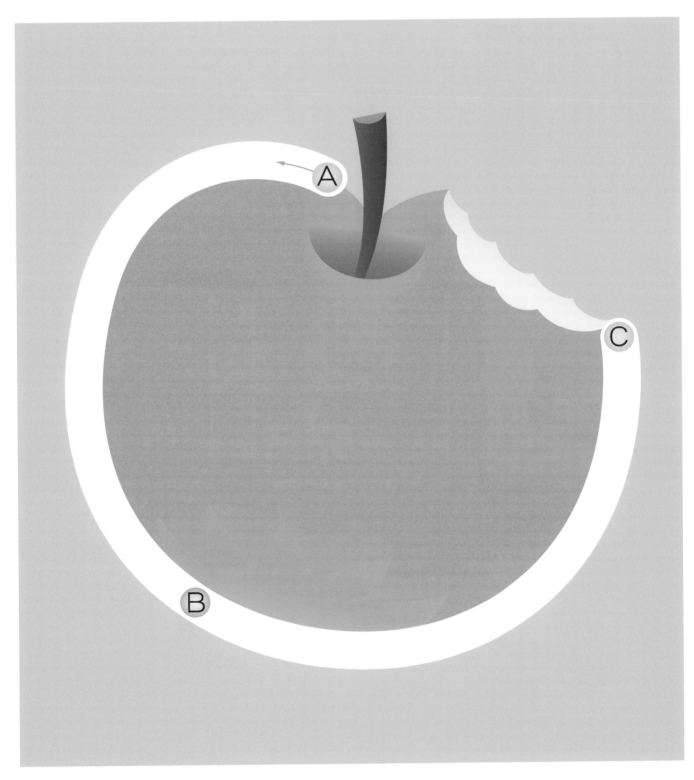

Writing "A·B·C"

■ Say the name of each letter. Then say the sound of the letter as you trace it. Follow the stroke order indicated by the numbers.

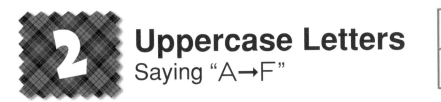

Uppercase Letters
Saying "A→F"

■ While saying each letter aloud, draw a line from "A" to "F"
  to connect the letters in alphabetical order.

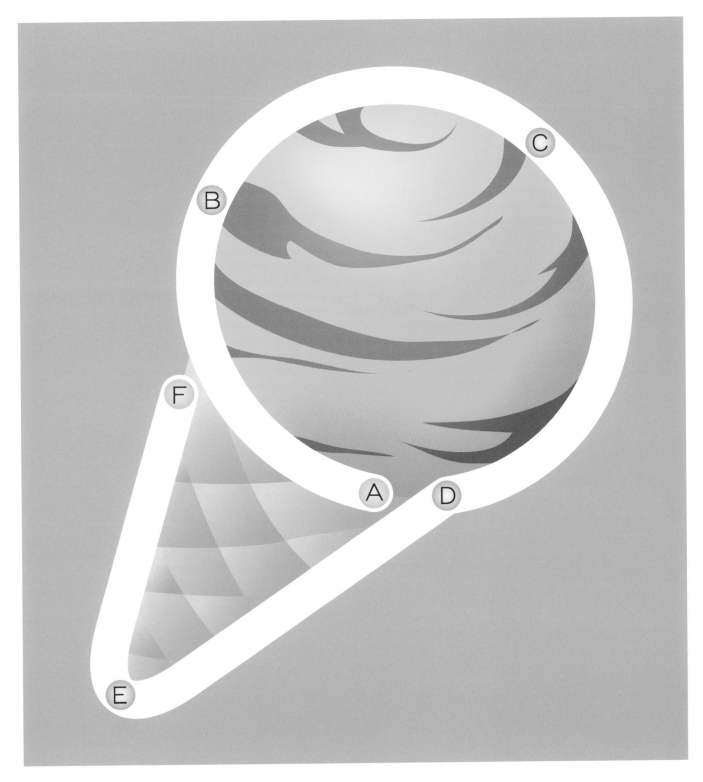

87

Writing "D·E·F"

■ Say the name of each letter. Then say the sound of the letter as you trace it. Follow the stroke order indicated by the numbers.

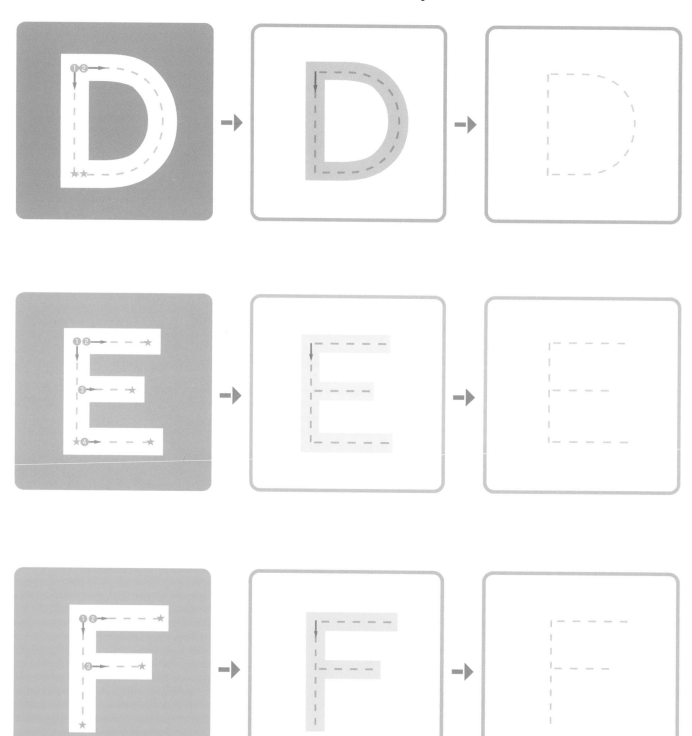

Uppercase Letters
Saying "A→I"

Name

Date

■ While saying each letter aloud, draw a line from "A" to "I" to connect the letters in alphabetical order.

Writing "G·H·I"

■ Say the name of each letter. Then say the sound of the letter as you trace it. Follow the stroke order indicated by the numbers.

Uppercase Letters

Saying "A→L"

Name

Date

■ While saying each letter aloud, draw a line from "A" to "L" to connect the letters in alphabetical order.

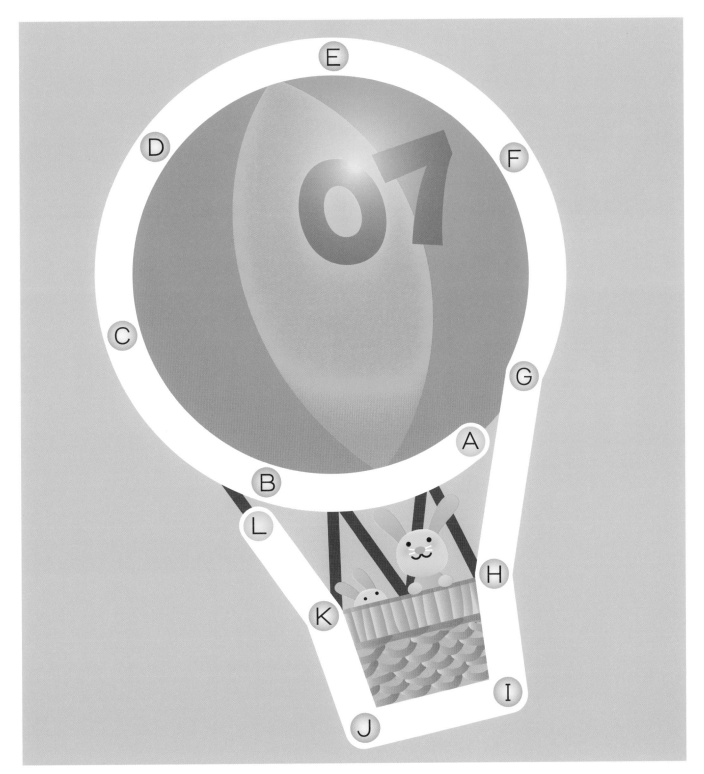

Writing "J·K·L"

■ Say the name of each letter. Then say the sound of the letter as you trace it. Follow the stroke order indicated by the numbers.

Uppercase Letters
Saying "A→O"

Name

Date

■ While saying each letter aloud, draw a line from "A" to "O" to connect the letters in alphabetical order.

Writing "M·N·O"

■ Say the name of each letter. Then say the sound of the letter as you trace it. Follow the stroke order indicated by the numbers.

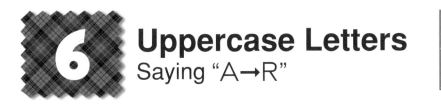

Uppercase Letters
Saying "A→R"

■ While saying each letter aloud, draw a line from "A" to "R" to connect the letters in alphabetical order.

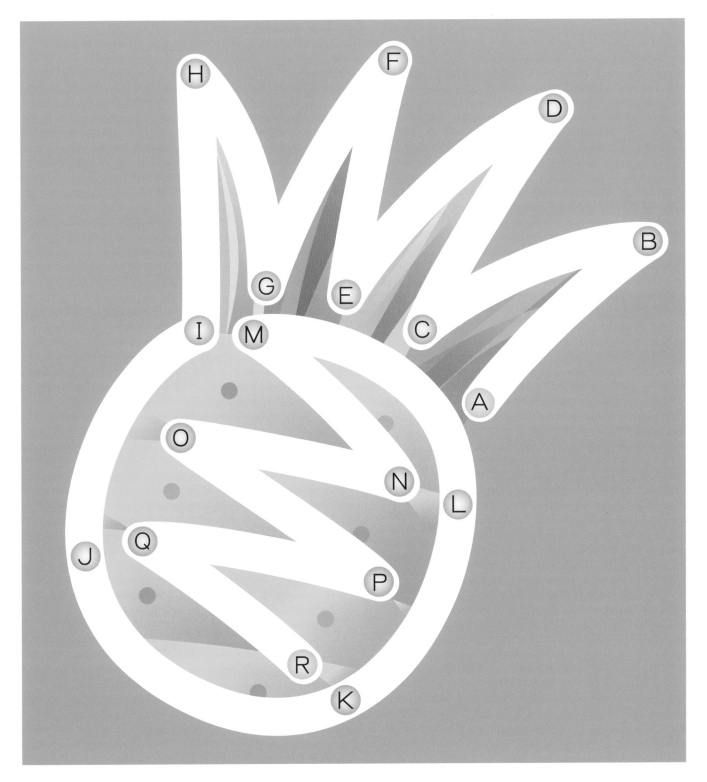

Writing "P·Q·R"

■ Say the name of each letter. Then say the sound of the letter as you trace it. Follow the stroke order indicated by the numbers.

Uppercase Letters
Saying "A→U"

Name	
Date	

■ While saying each letter aloud, draw a line from "A" to "U" to connect the letters in alphabetical order.

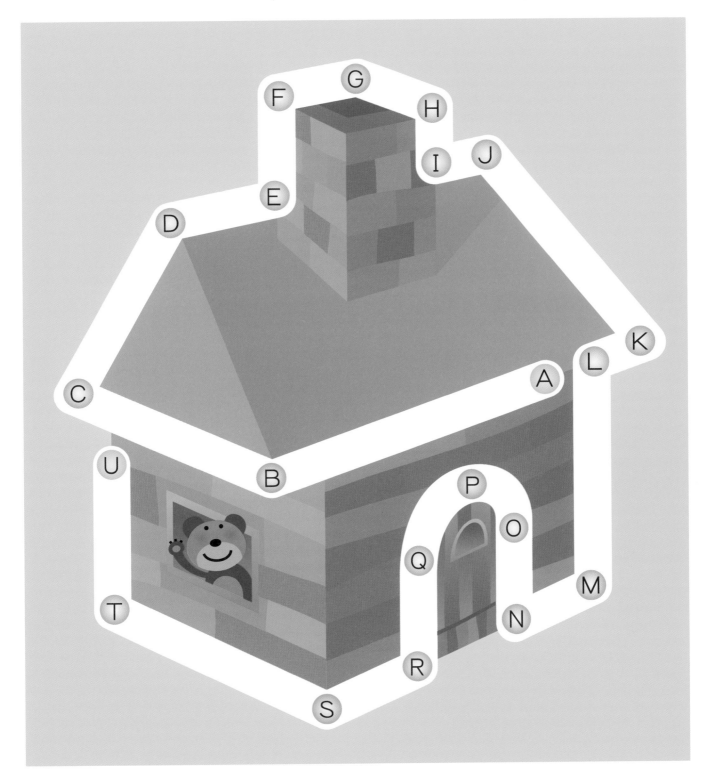

Writing "S·T·U"

■ Say the name of each letter. Then say the sound of the letter as you trace it. Follow the stroke order indicated by the numbers.

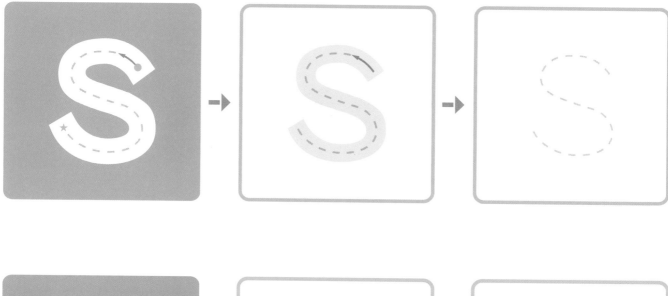

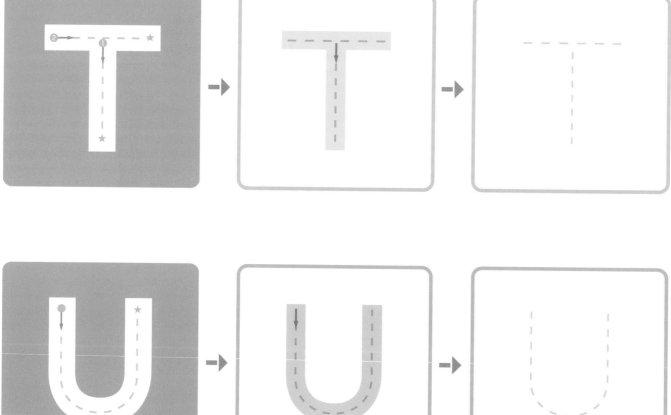

8

Uppercase Letters
Saying "A→X"

■ While saying each letter aloud, draw a line from "A" to "X"
  to connect the letters in alphabetical order.

Writing "V·W·X"

■ Say the name of each letter. Then say the sound of the letter as you trace it. Follow the stroke order indicated by the numbers.

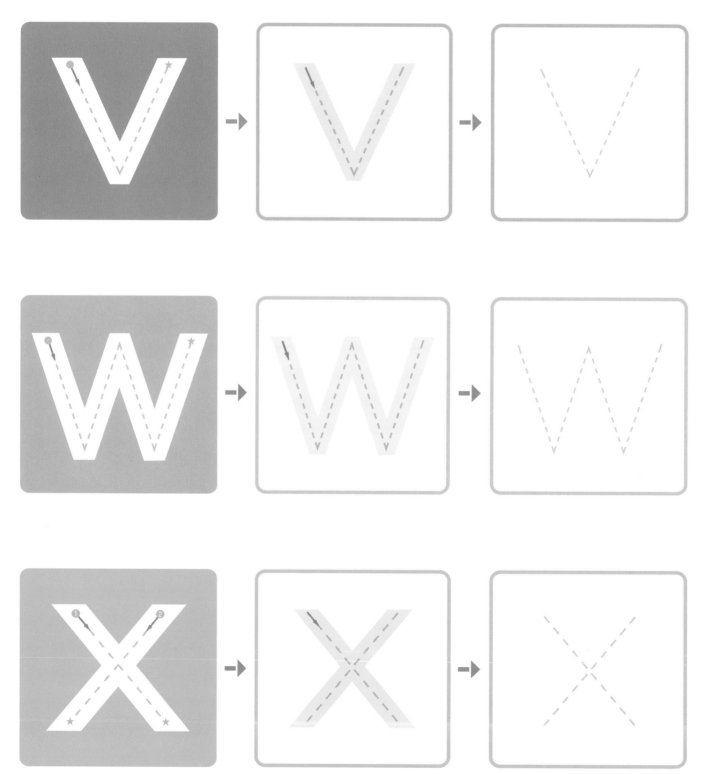

■ While saying each letter aloud, draw a line from "A" to "Z" to connect the letters in alphabetical order.

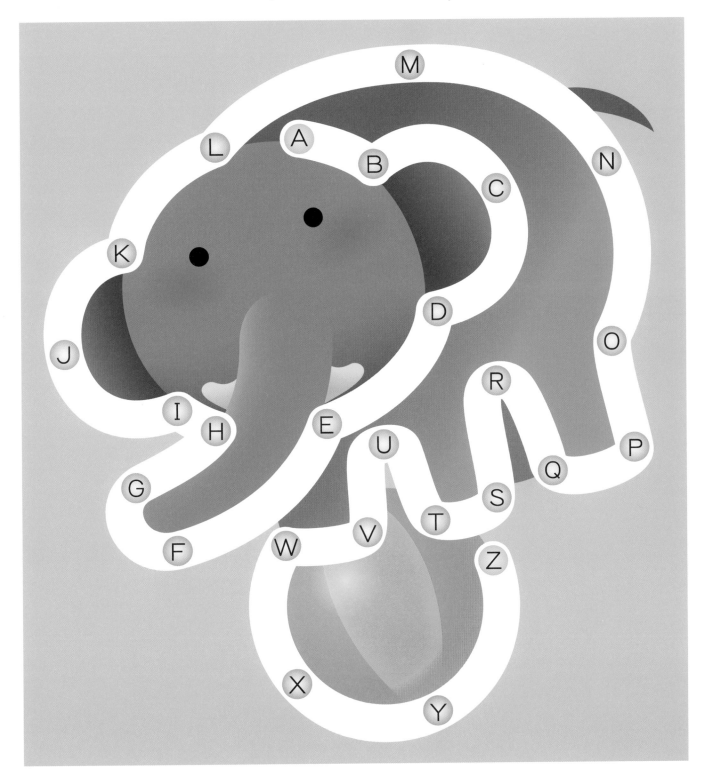

Writing "Y·Z"

■Say the name of each letter. Then say the sound of the letter as you trace it. Follow the stroke order indicated by the numbers.

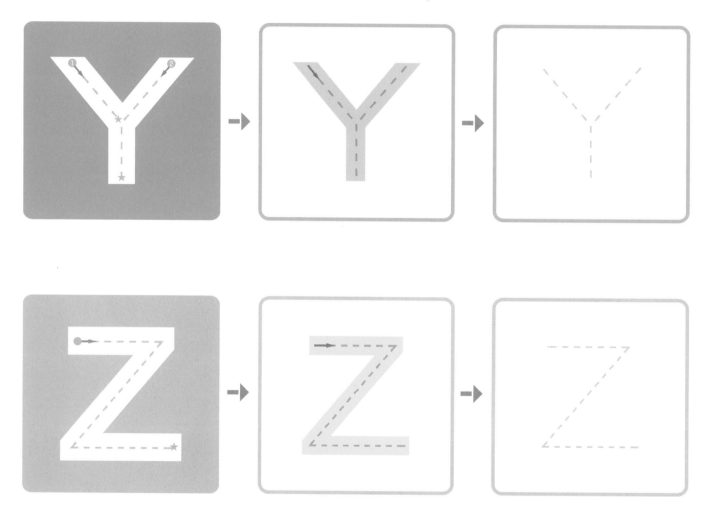

Lowercase Letters
Saying "a·b·c"

Name

Date

To parents
On this page, your child will connect the first three lowercase letters of the alphabet. From this page on, the number of letters will gradually increase. Please have your child say the letters aloud while he or she is connecting the dots. The answer to each puzzle can be found at the bottom of the following page.

■ While saying each letter aloud, draw a line from "a" to "c" to connect the letters in alphabetical order.

Writing "a·b·c"

■ Say the name of each letter. Then say the sound of the letter as you trace it. Follow the stroke order indicated by the numbers.

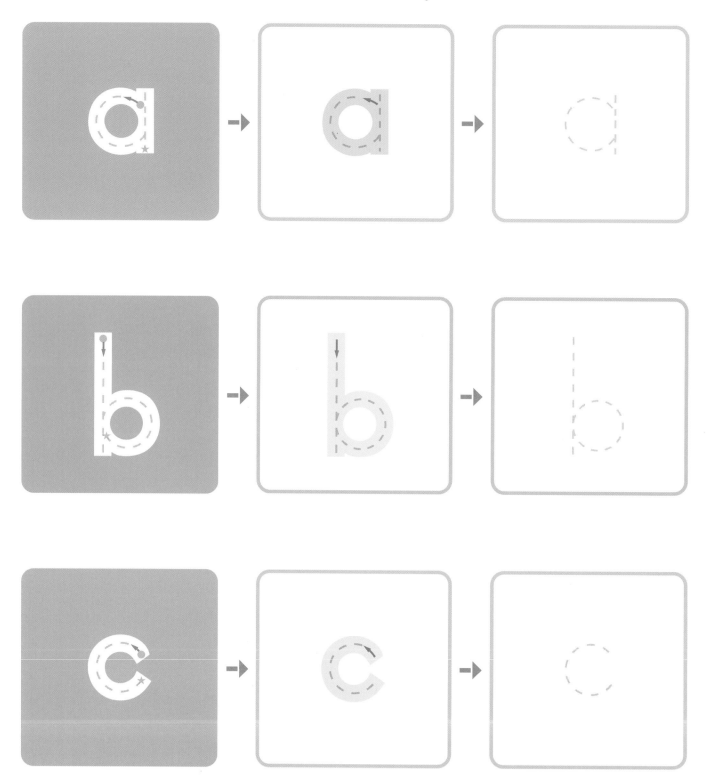

(P103 Answer - fish)

Lowercase Letters
Saying "a → f"

Name

Date

■ While saying each letter aloud, draw a line from "a" to "f" to connect the letters in alphabetical order.

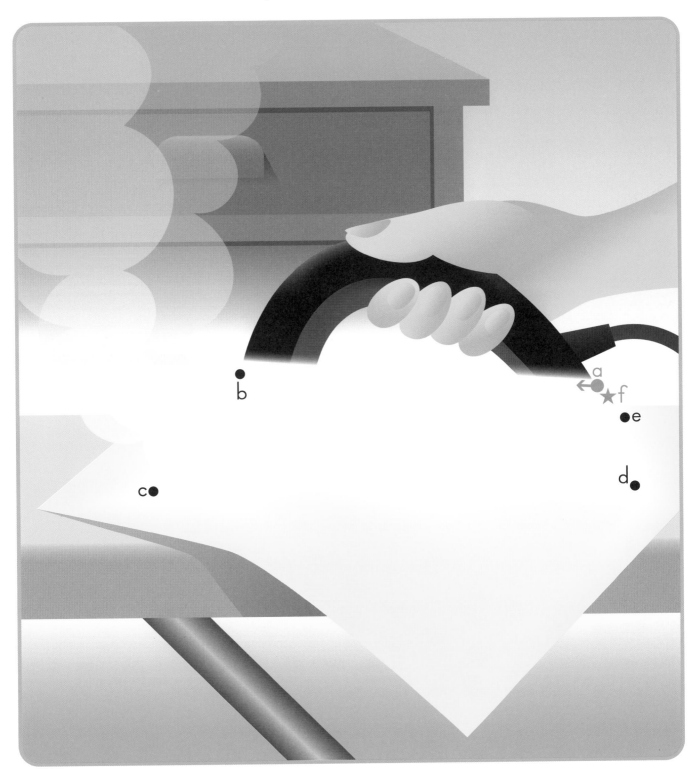

Writing "d.e.f"

■ Say the name of each letter. Then say the sound of the letter as you trace it. Follow the stroke order indicated by the numbers.

(P105 Answer - iron)

Lowercase Letters
Saying "a → i"

Name

Date

■ While saying each letter aloud, draw a line from "a" to "i" to connect the letters in alphabetical order.

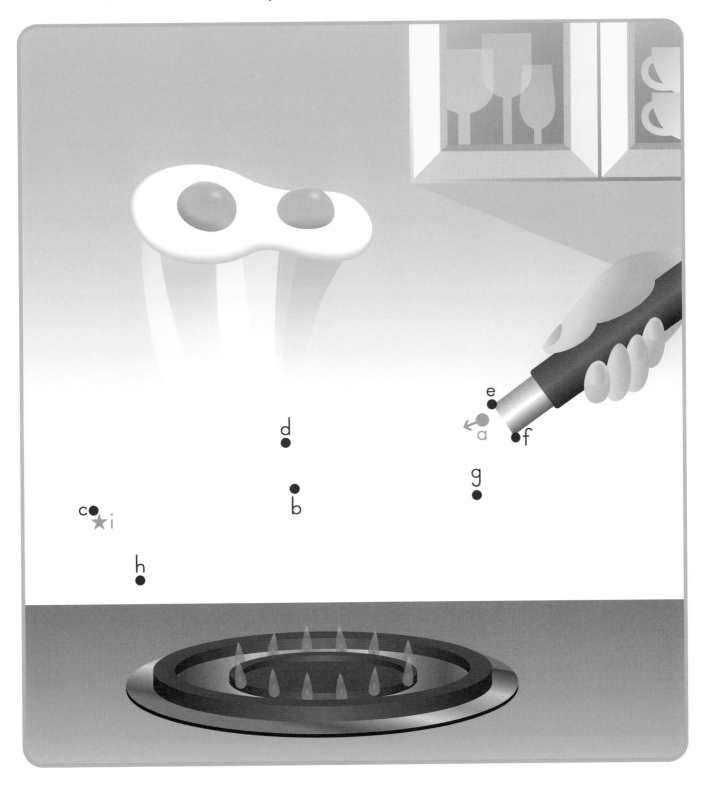

Writing "g·h·i"

■ Say the name of each letter. Then say the sound of the letter as you trace it. Follow the stroke order indicated by the numbers.

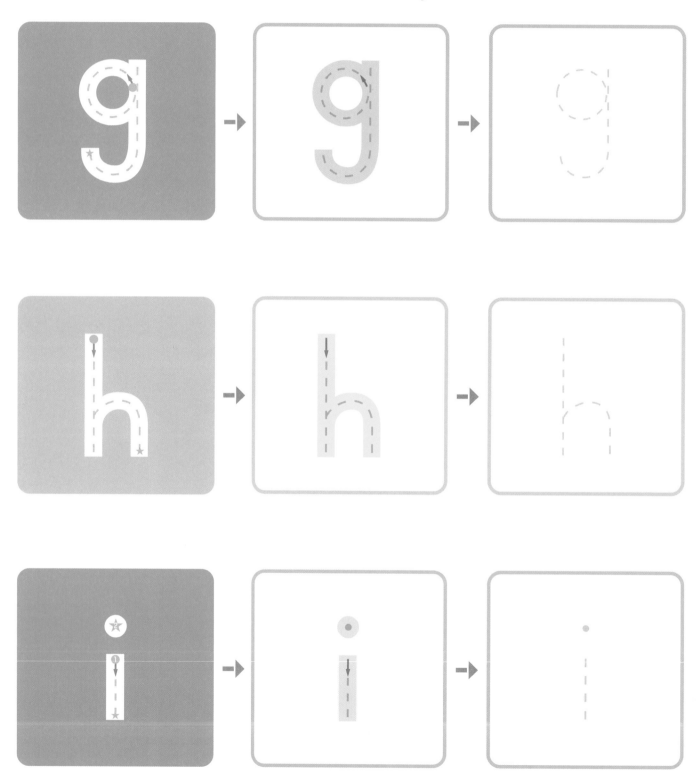

(P107 Answer - frying pan)

Name

Date

■ While saying each letter aloud, draw a line from "a" to "l" to connect the letters in alphabetical order.

Writing "j·k·l"

■ Say the name of each letter. Then say the sound of the letter as you trace it. Follow the stroke order indicated by the numbers.

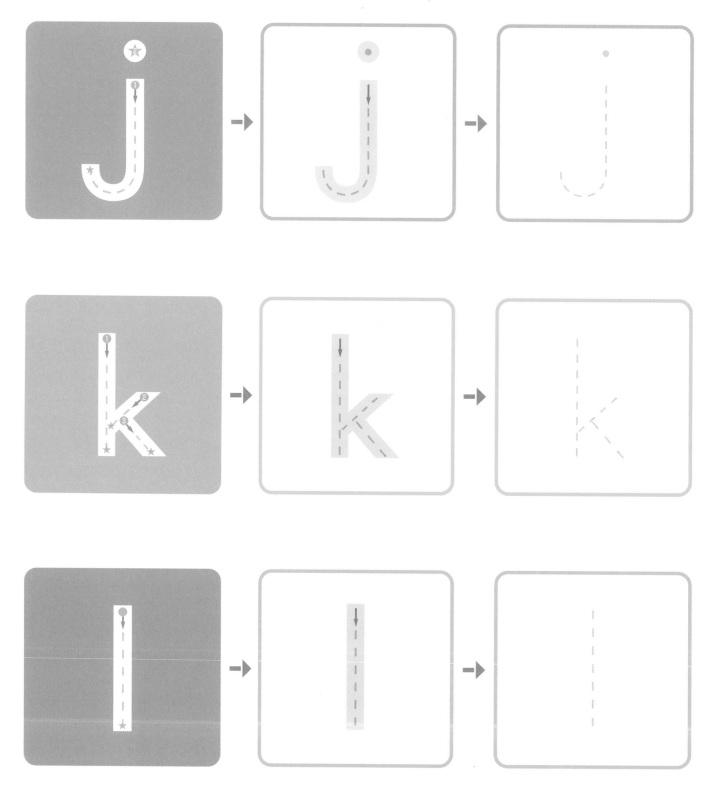

(P109 Answer - cap)

14

Lowercase Letters
Saying "a → o"

■ While saying each letter aloud, draw a line from "a" to "o" to connect the letters in alphabetical order.

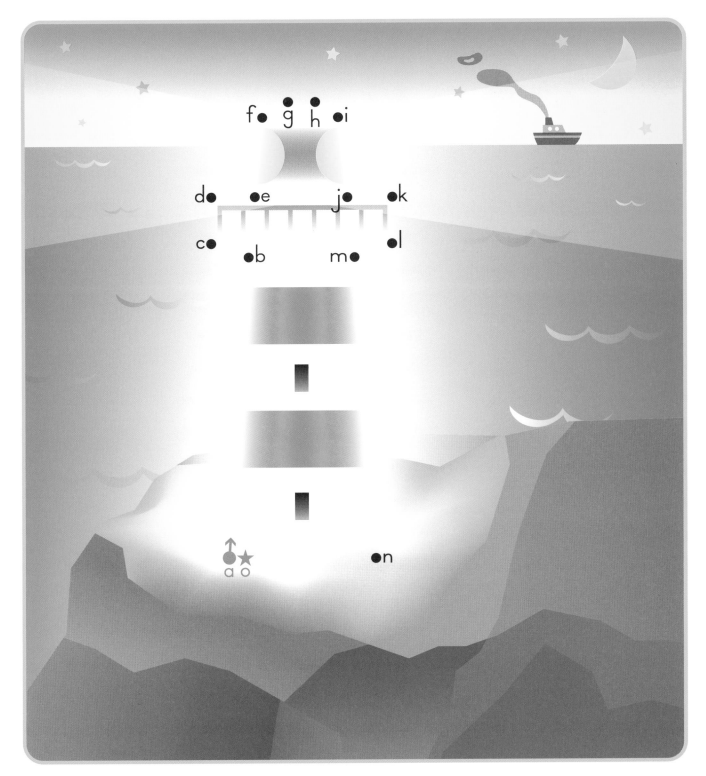

Writing "m·n·o"

■ Say the name of each letter. Then say the sound of the letter as you trace it. Follow the stroke order indicated by the numbers.

(P111 Answer - lighthouse)

15

Lowercase Letters
Saying "a → r"

Name

Date

■ While saying each letter aloud, draw a line from "a" to "r" to connect the letters in alphabetical order.

Writing "p·q·r"

■ Say the name of each letter. Then say the sound of the letter as you trace it. Follow the stroke order indicated by the numbers.

(P113 Answer - juice)

Lowercase Letters
Saying "a → u"

Name

Date

■ While saying each letter aloud, draw a line from "a" to "u" to connect the letters in alphabetical order.

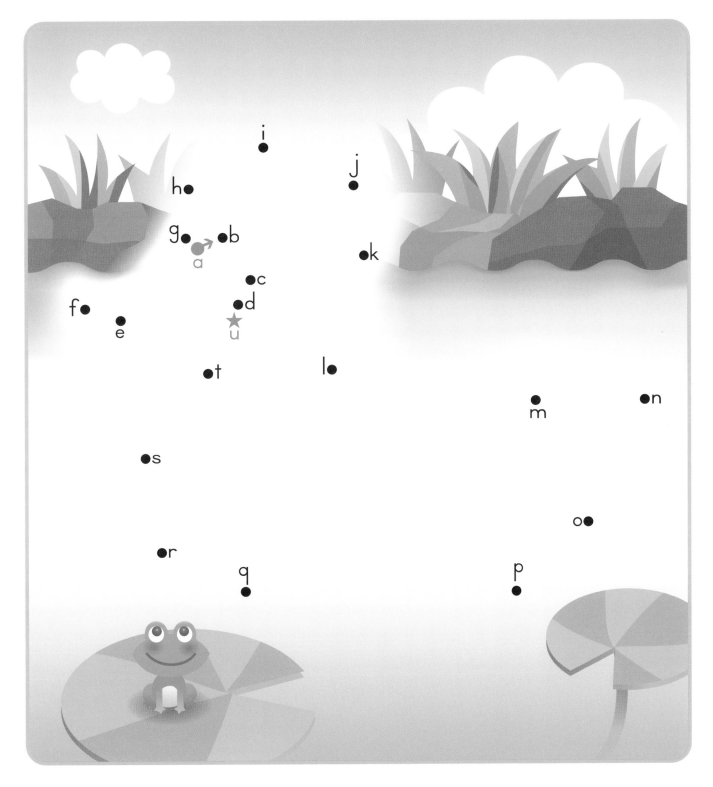

Writing "s·t·u"

■ Say the name of each letter. Then say the sound of the letter as you trace it. Follow the stroke order indicated by the numbers.

(P115 Answer - duck)

Lowercase Letters
Saying "a → x"

■ While saying each letter aloud, draw a line from "a" to "x" to connect the letters in alphabetical order.

Writing "v·w·x"

■ Say the name of each letter. Then say the sound of the letter as you trace it. Follow the stroke order indicated by the numbers.

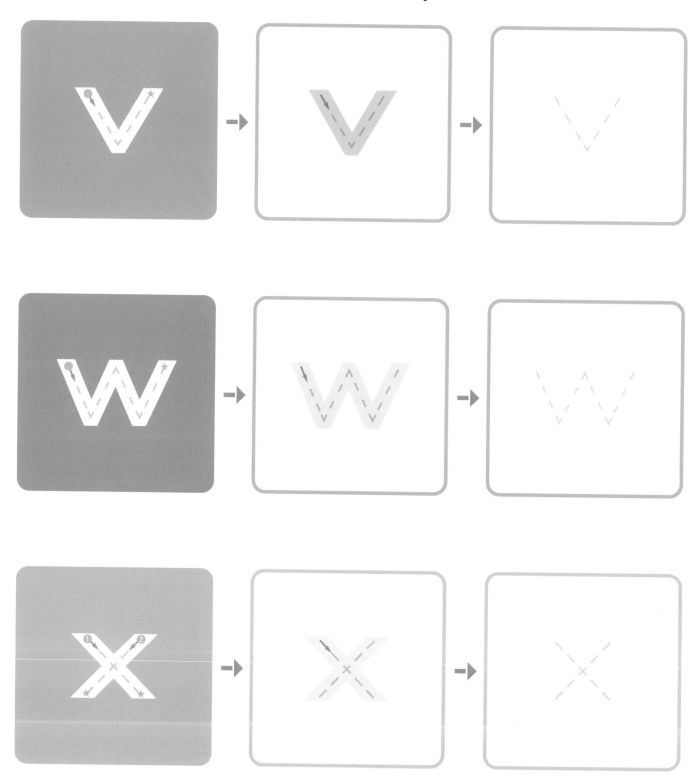

(P117 Answer - tulip)

118

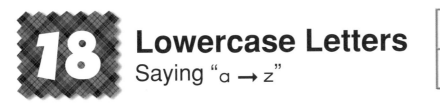

18 Lowercase Letters
Saying "a → z"

Name

Date

■ While saying each letter aloud, draw a line from "a" to "z" to connect the letters in alphabetical order.

119

Writing "y·z"

■ Say the name of each letter. Then say the sound of the letter as you trace it. Follow the stroke order indicated by the numbers.

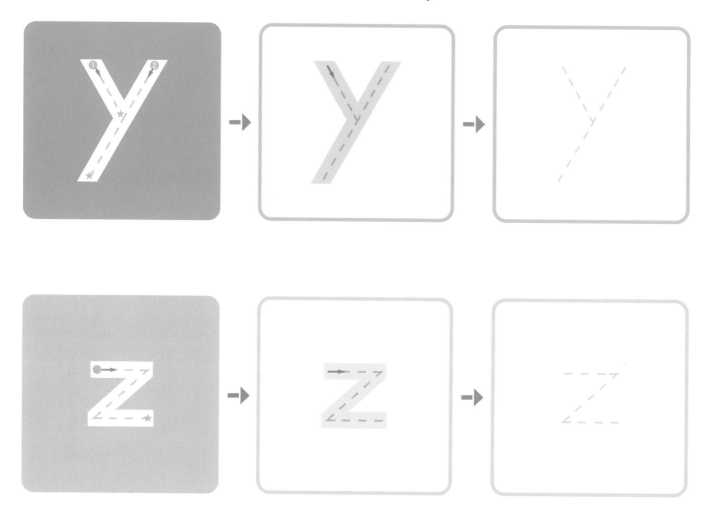

(P119 Answer - bulldog)

Name

Date

■ Trace the letters "A" to "Z" while saying each letter aloud.

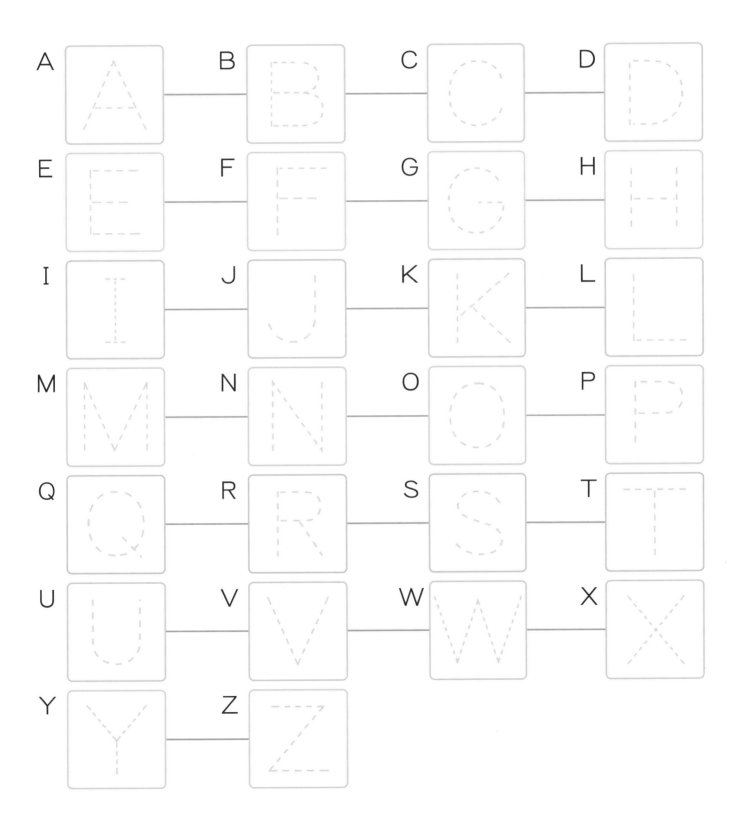

A B C D

E F G H

I J K L

M N O P

Q R S T

U V W X

Y Z

Writing "a → z"

■ Trace the letters "a" to "z" while saying each letter aloud.

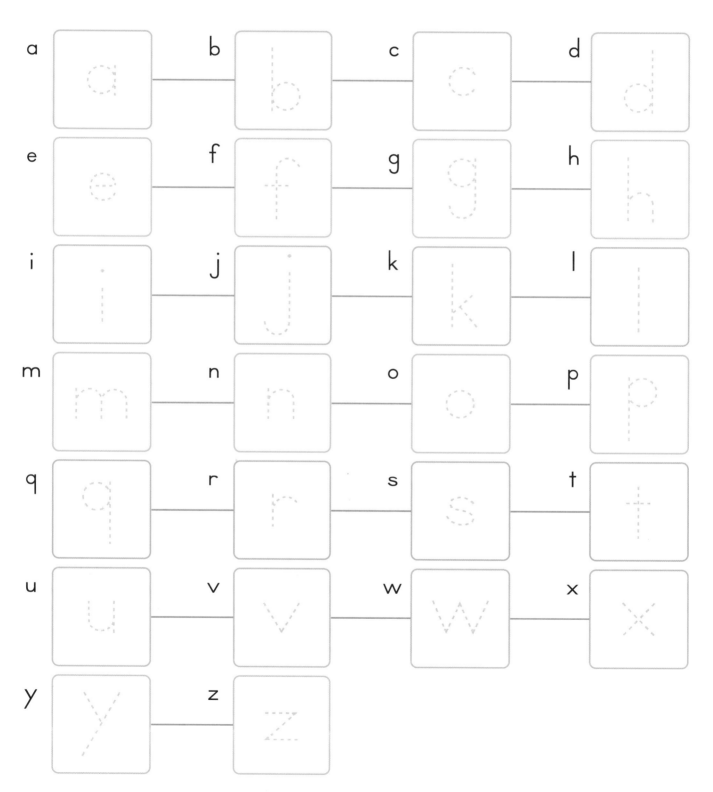

Upper- and Lower-case Letters
Writing "A·a / B·b"

Name

Date

To parents
In this exercise, your child will practice linking uppercase letters to their lowercase counterparts. Please help your child read the names of the characters. Then point out that each pair of words start with the same letter–one uppercase and one lowercase.

■ Look at the first letters of the words below. Then trace the letters.

Anna   ant

Anna   ant

Bob   bat

Bob   bat

Writing "A·a / B·b"

■ Trace and then write each letter while saying it aloud.

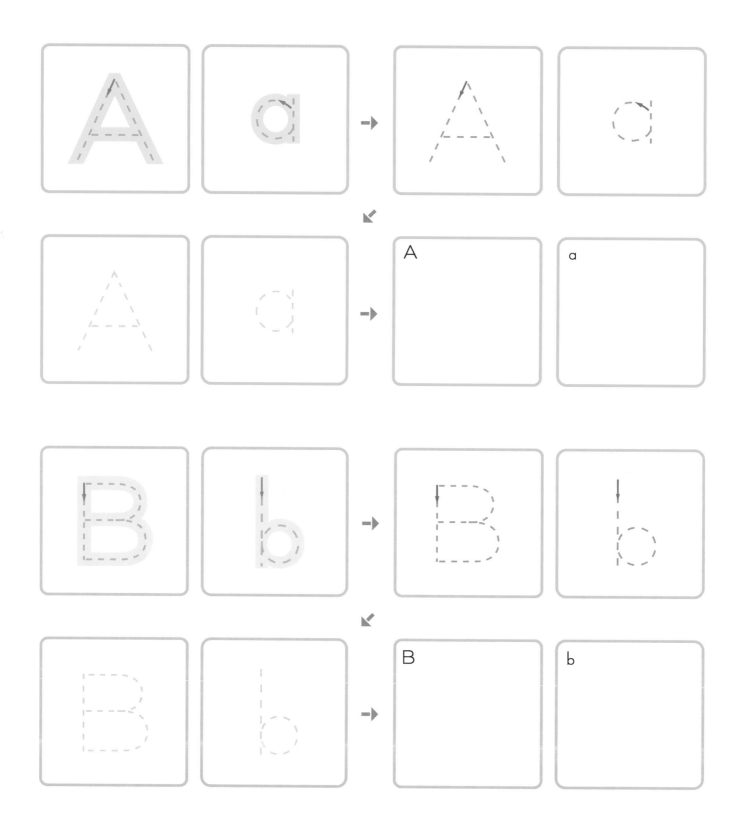

■ Look at the first letters of the words below. Then trace the letters.

Cam   cow

Cam   Cow

Dan   dog

Dan   dog

Writing "C·c/D·d"

■ Trace and then write each letter while saying it aloud.

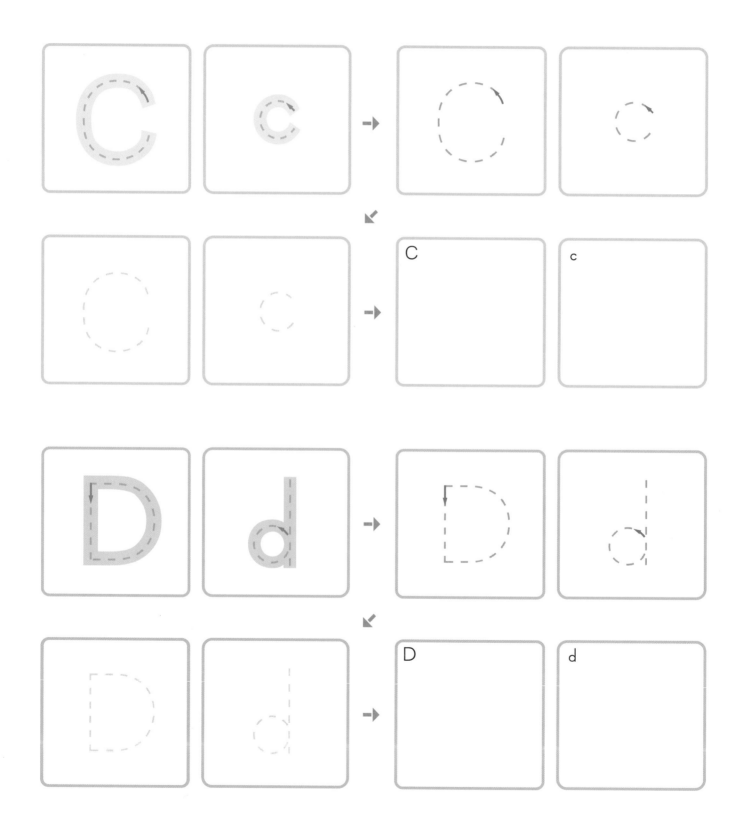

Name

Date

■ Trace each letter while saying it aloud.

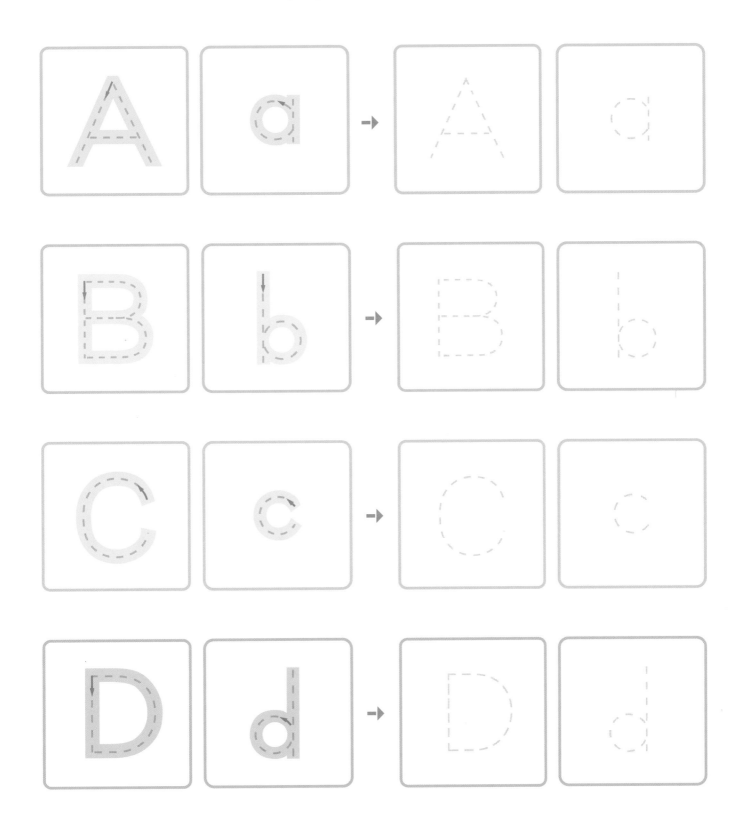

Writing "A·a → D·d"

■ Trace and then write each letter while saying it aloud.

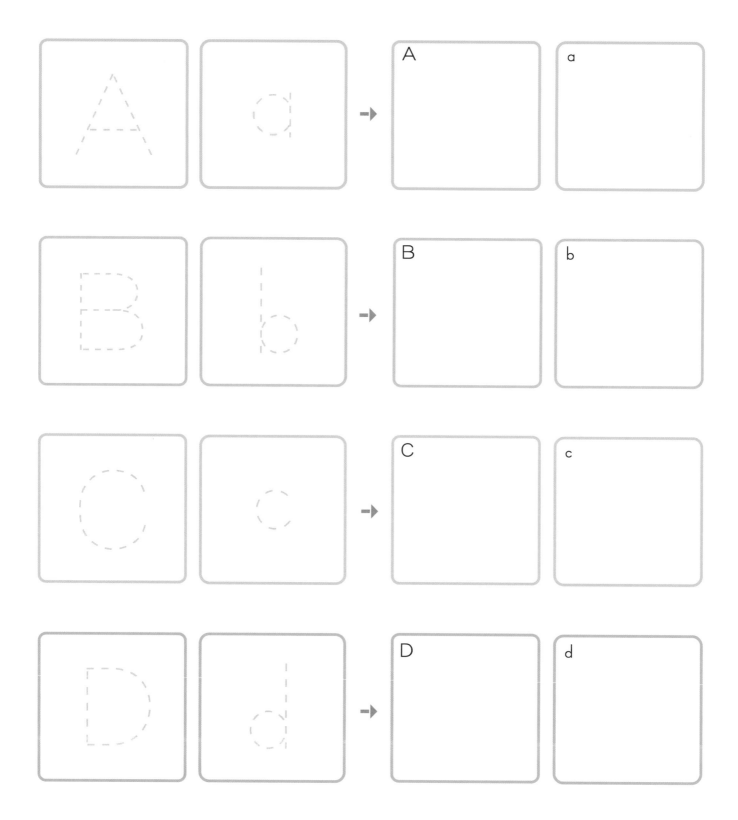

Name

Date

■ Look at the first letters of the words below. Then trace the letters.

Ed   elephant

Ed elephant

Fred   fox

Fred fox

Writing "E·e / F· f"

■ Trace and then write each letter while saying it aloud.

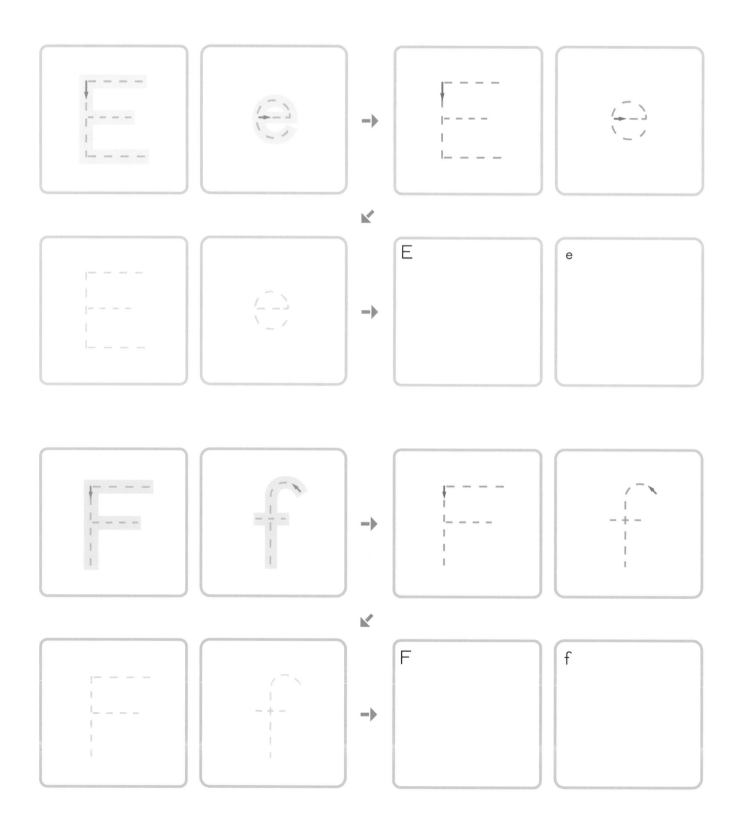

Name

Date

■ Look at the first letters of the words below. Then trace the letters.

Gus   goat   Gus   goat

Hal   hippo   Hal   hippo

Writing "G·g/H·h"

■ Trace and then write each letter while saying it aloud.

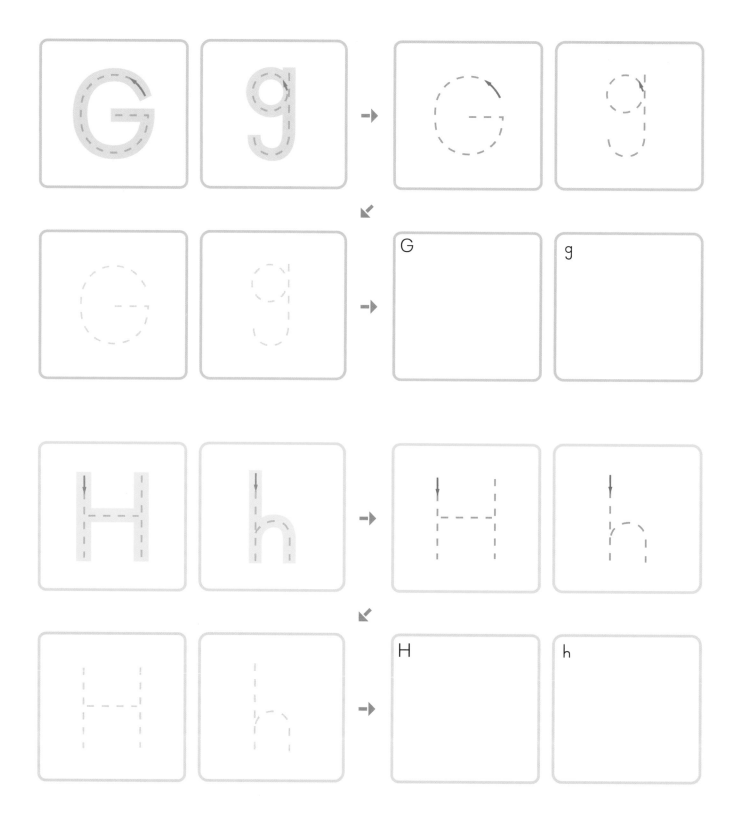

Review

Writing "E·e → H·h"

Name
Date

■ Trace each letter while saying it aloud.

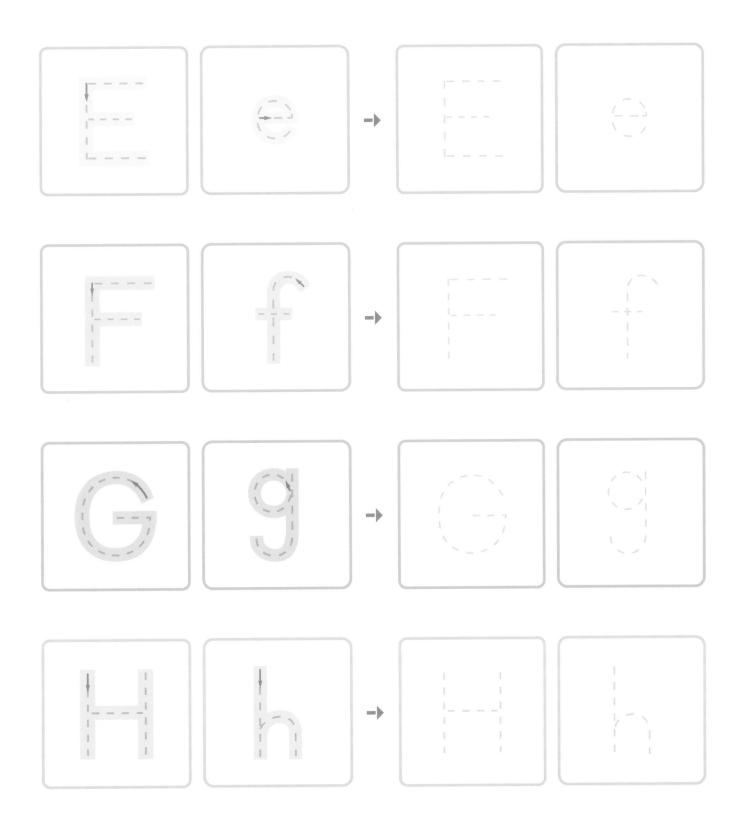

Writing "E·e→H·h"

■ Trace and then write each letter while saying it aloud.

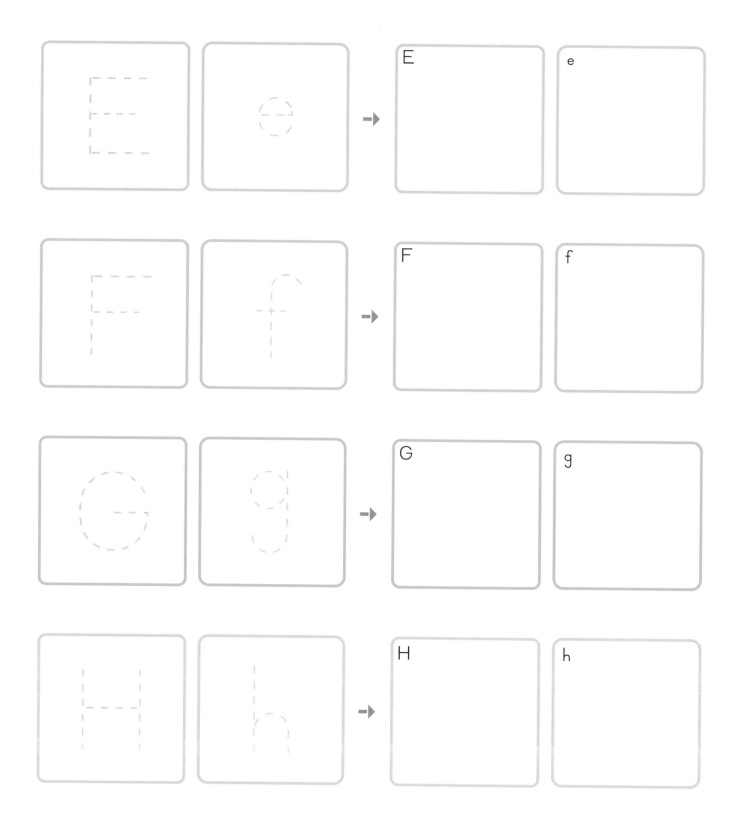

26 Upper- and Lower-case Letters

Writing "I·i / J·j"

■ Look at the first letters of the words below. Then trace the letters.

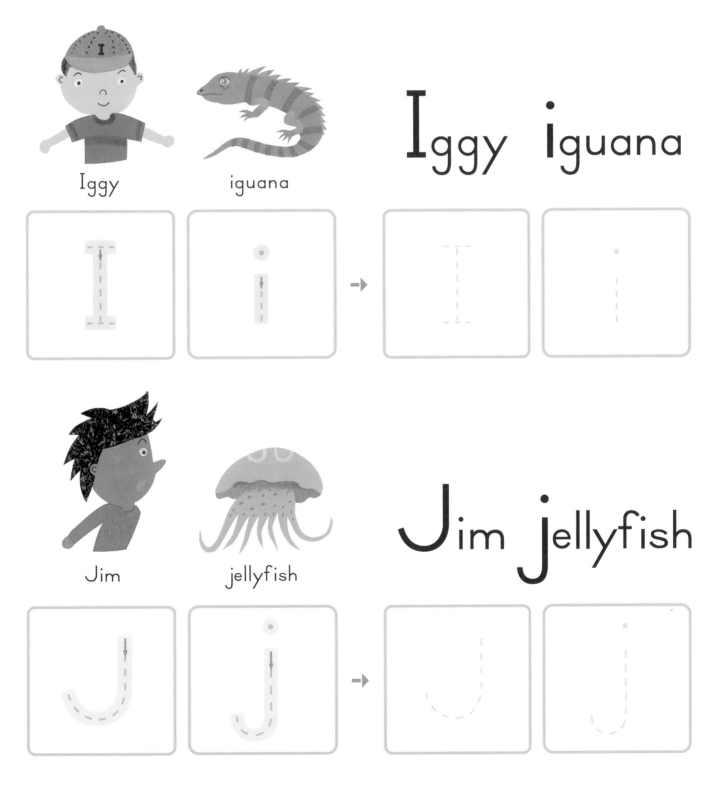

Iggy   iguana

Iggy

iguana

Jim   jellyfish

Jim

jellyfish

Writing "I·i / J·j"

■ Trace and then write each letter while saying it aloud.

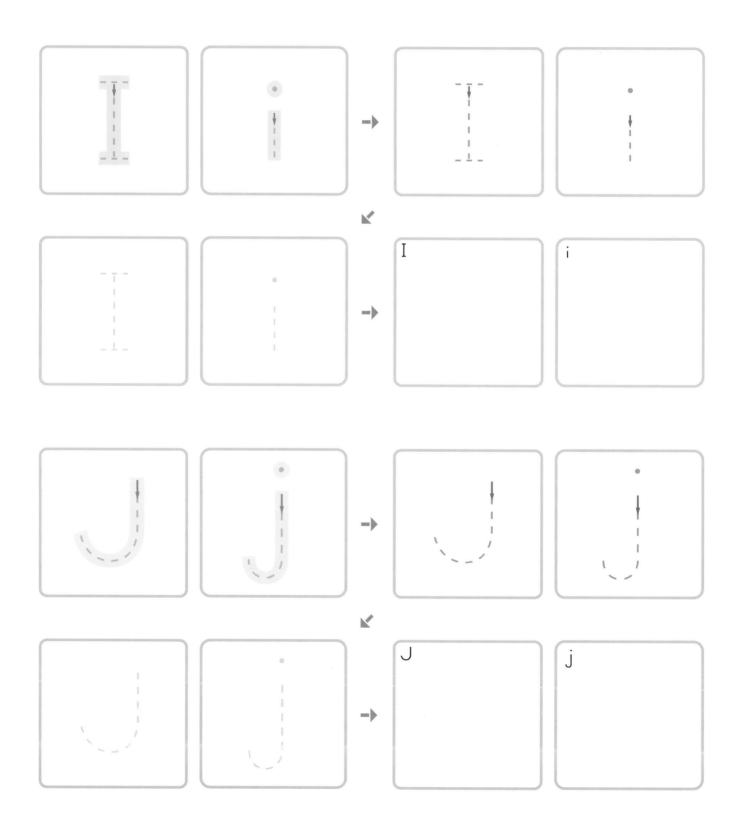

Name

Date

■ Look at the first letters of the words below. Then trace the letters.

Kim   kitten

Kim   kitten

K   k   →   K   k

Larry   lion

Larry   lion

L   l   →

Writing "K·k / L·l"

■ Trace and then write each letter while saying it aloud.

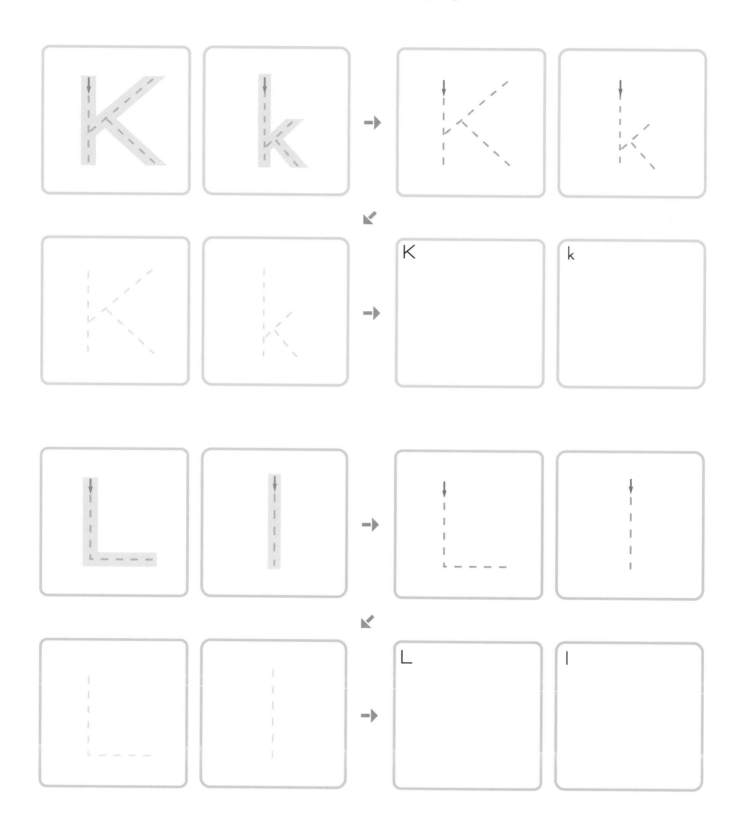

Review

Writing "I·i → L·l"

Name

Date

■ Trace each letter while saying it aloud.

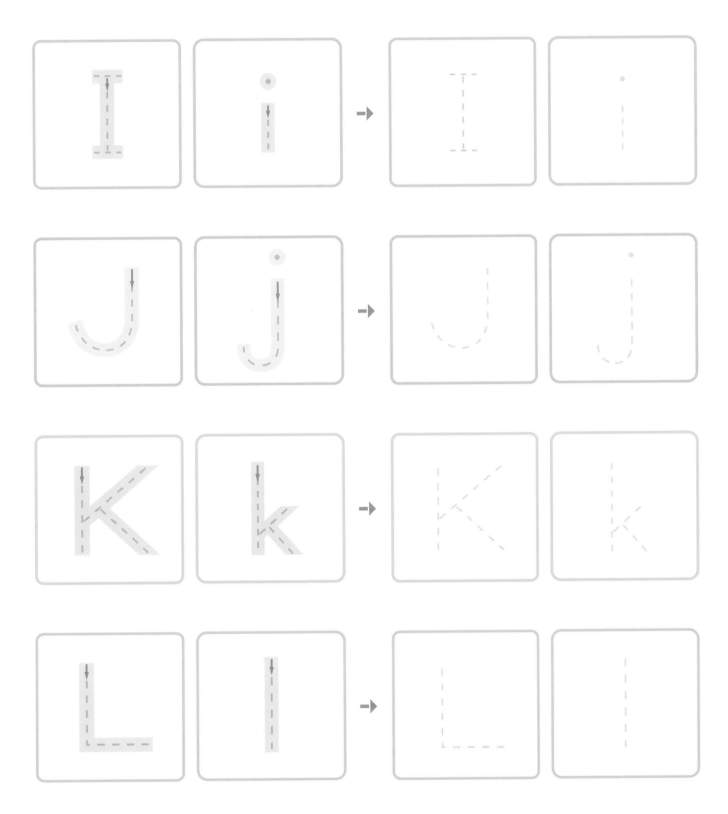

Writing "I·i → L·l"

■ Trace and then write each letter while saying it aloud.

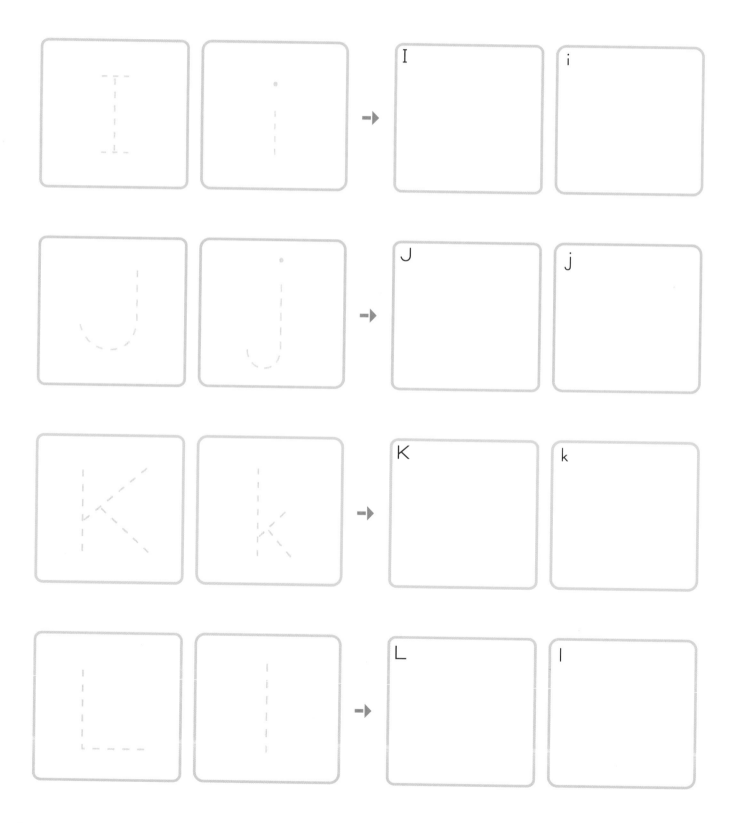

Name

Date

■ Look at the first letters of the words below. Then trace the letters.

Matt moose

Matt

moose

M m → M m

Nan newt

Nan

newt

N n → N n

Writing "M·m / N·n"

■ Trace and then write each letter while saying it aloud.

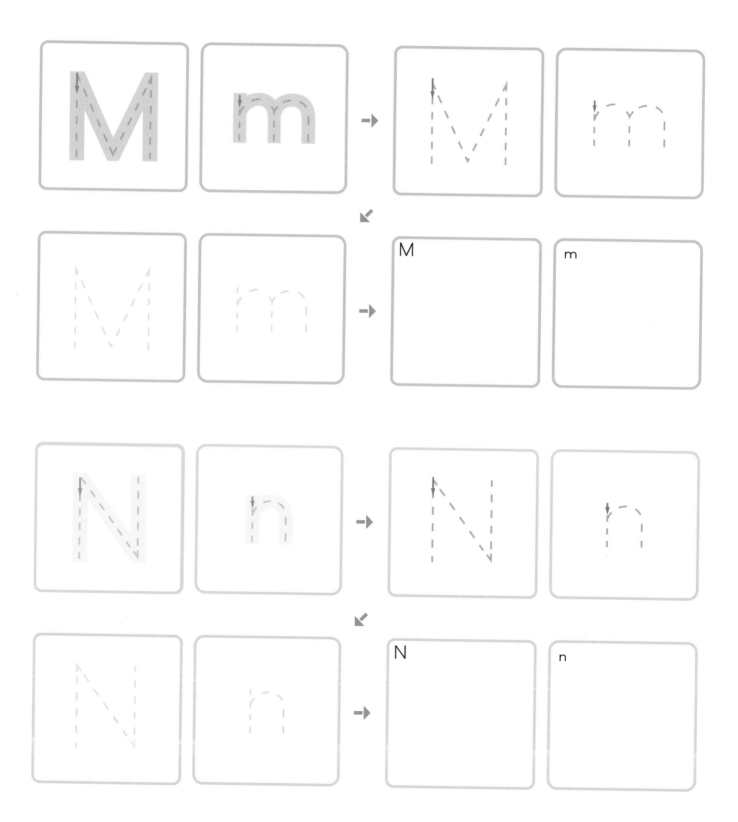

Name

Date

■ Look at the first letters of the words below. Then trace the letters.

Olly

octopus

Olly Octopus

Polly

pig

Polly pig

Writing "O·o / P·p"

■ Trace and then write each letter while saying it aloud.

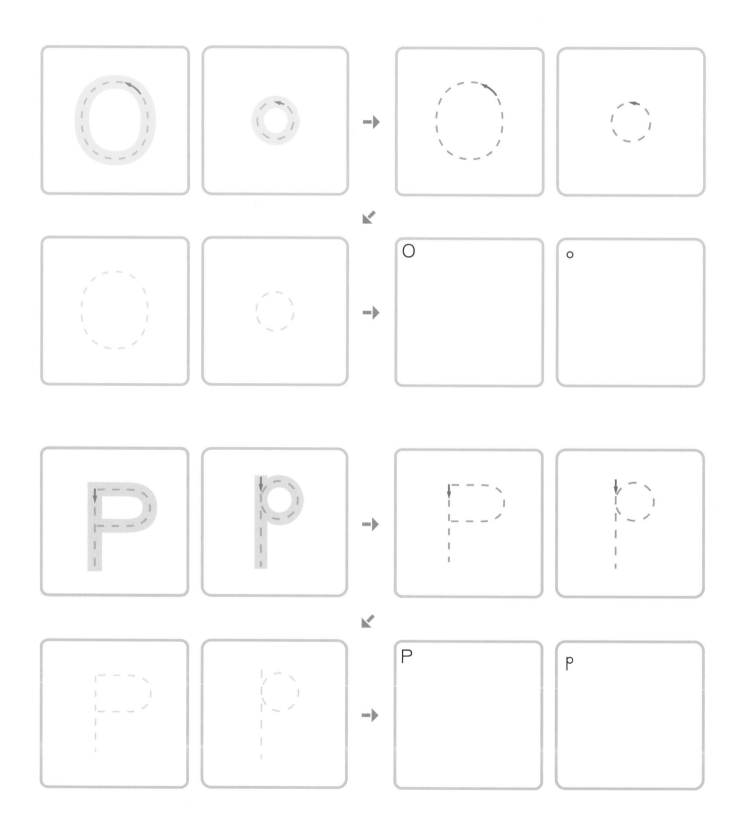

Name

Date

■ Trace each letter while saying it aloud.

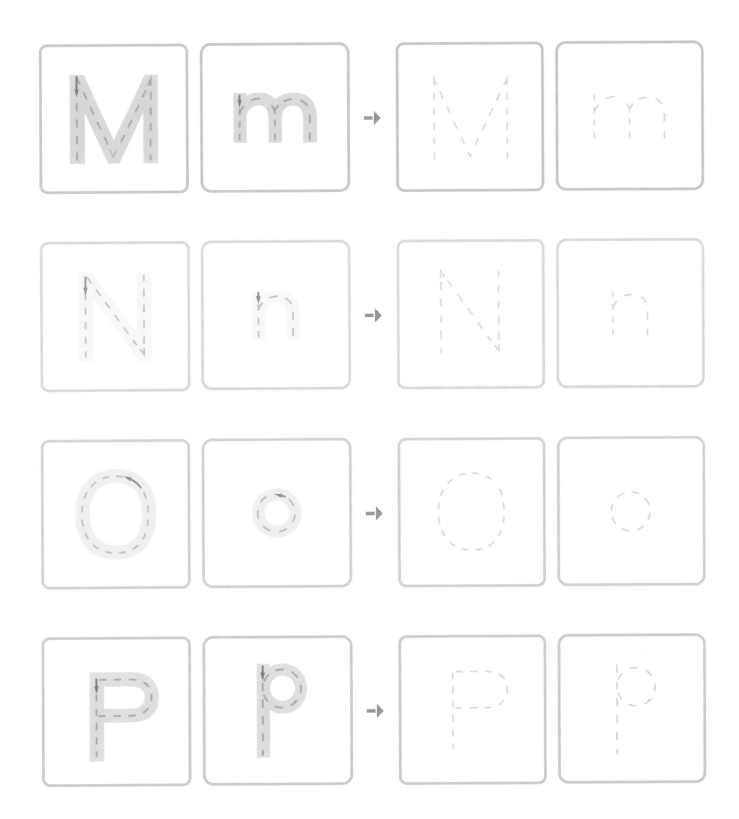

Writing "M·m → P·p"

■ Trace and then write each letter while saying it aloud.

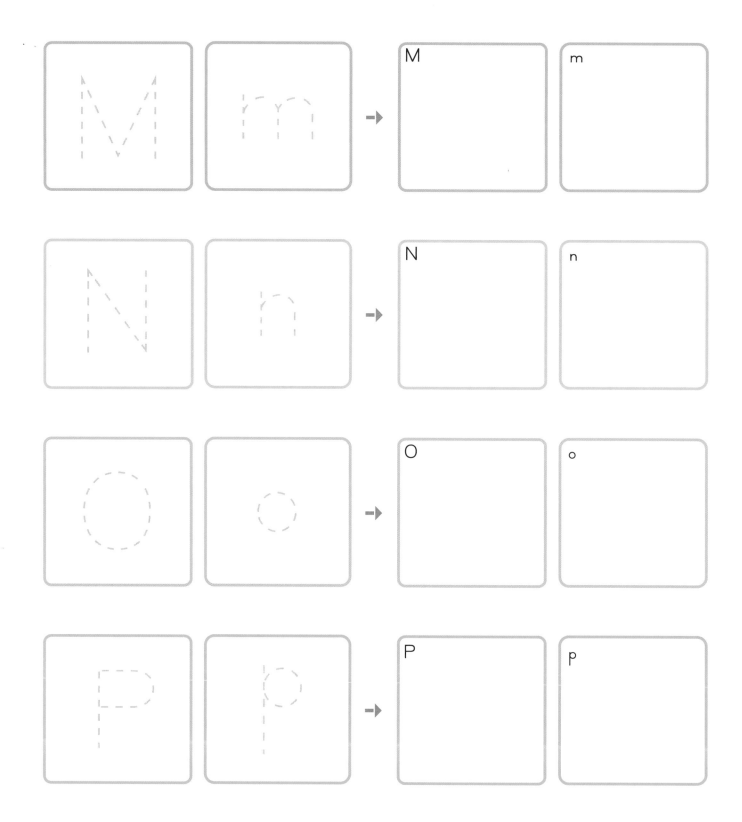

32 Upper- and Lower-case Letters
Writing "Q·q/R·r"

Name

Date

■ Look at the first letters of the words below. Then trace the letters.

Quinn quail

Quinn

quail

Rob rooster

Rob

rooster

Writing "Q·q/R·r"

■ Trace and then write each letter while saying it aloud.

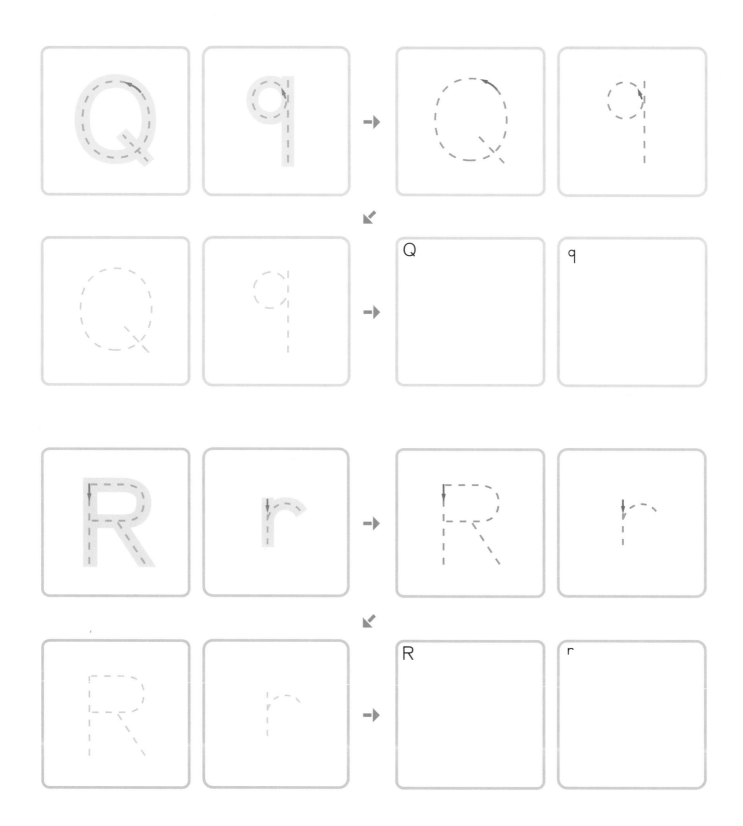

Name

Date

■ Look at the first letters of the words below. Then trace the letters.

Sal

snail

Sal Snail

Tim

tiger

Tim tiger

Writing "S·s / T·t"

■ Trace and then write each letter while saying it aloud.

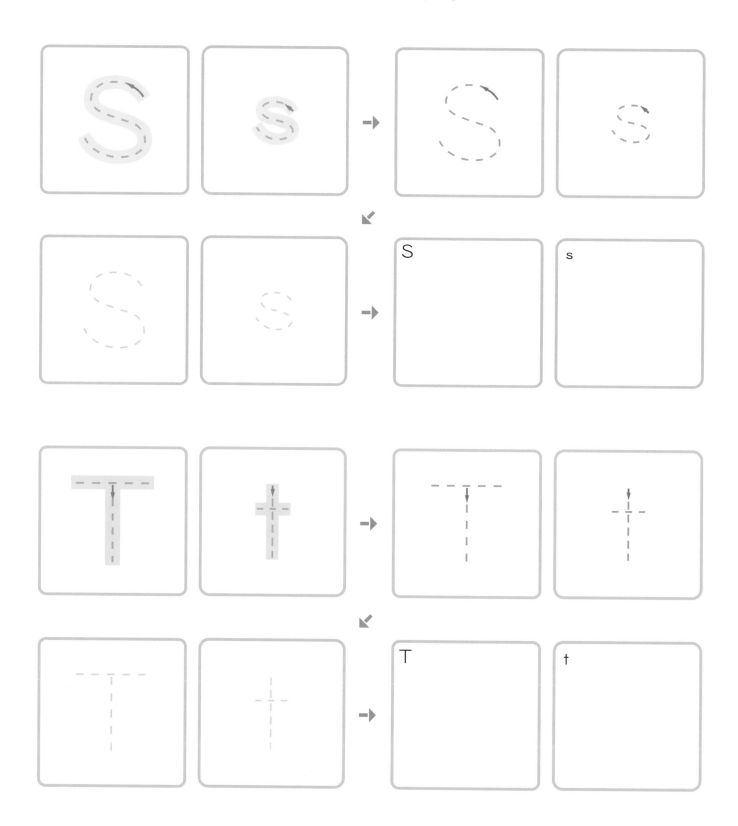

Name

Date

■ Trace each letter while saying it aloud.

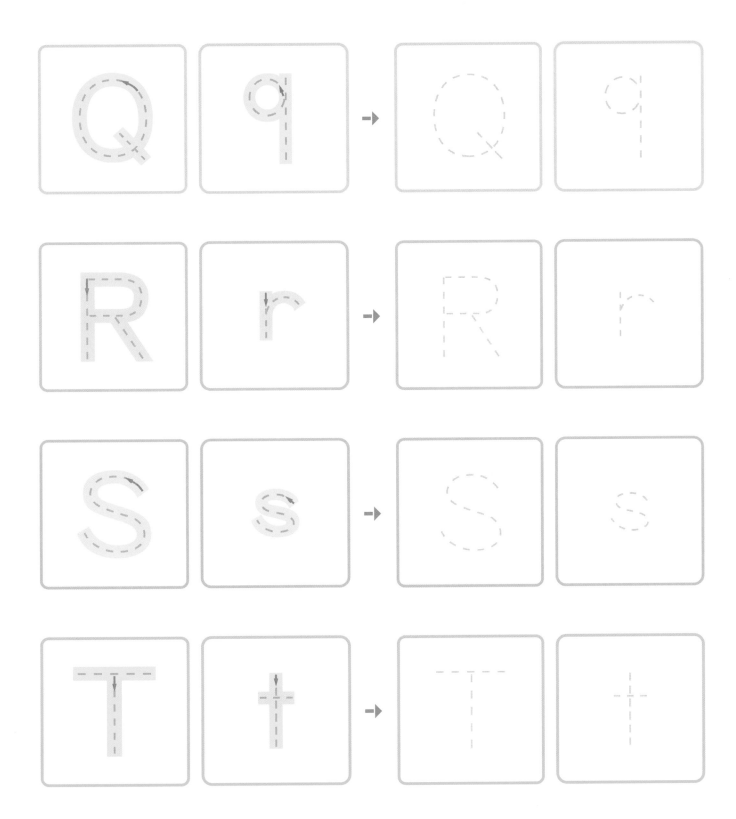

Writing "Q·q → T·t"

■ Trace and then write each letter while saying it aloud.

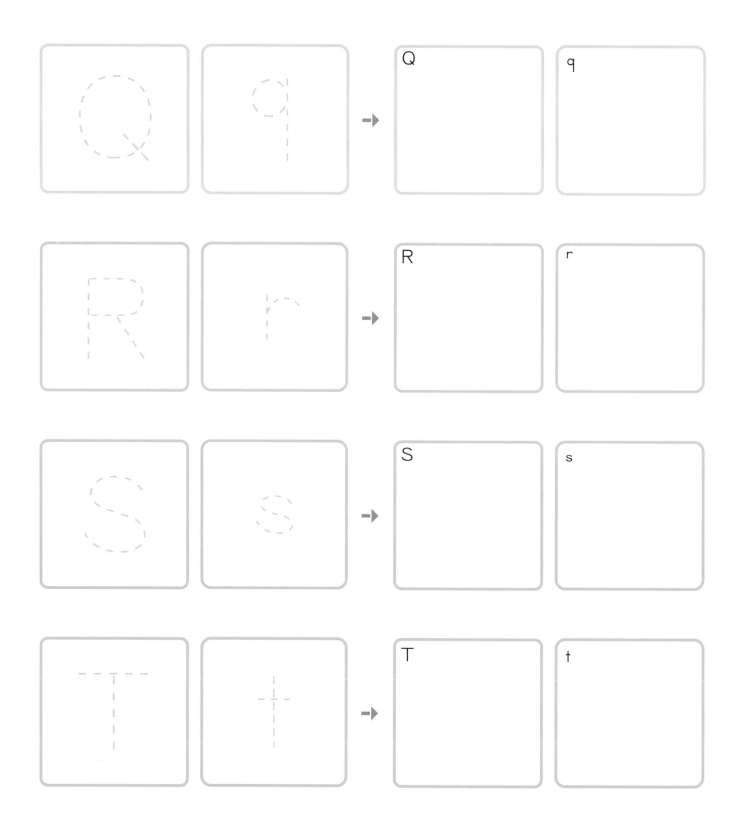

Upper- and Lower-case Letters
Writing "U·u / V·v"

■ Look at the first letters of the words below. Then trace the letters.

Uma   unicorn

Uma Unicorn

Vic   vulture

Vic Vulture

Writing "U·u / V·v"

■ Trace and then write each letter while saying it aloud.

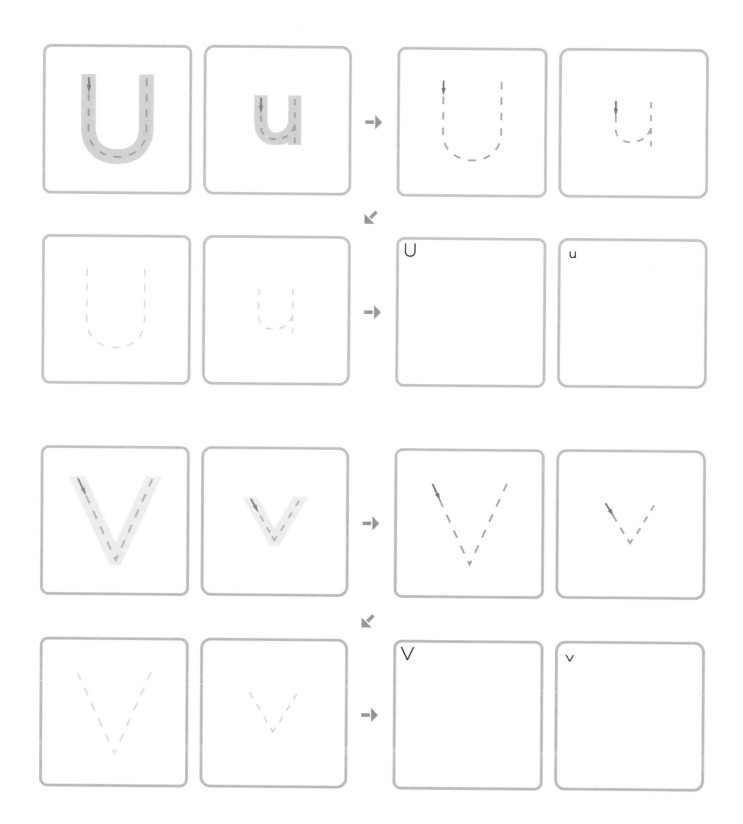

Upper- and Lower-case Letters

Writing "W·w/X·x"

Name

Date

■ Look at the first letters of the words below. Then trace the letters.

Will   walrus

Will **W**alrus

Xena   ox

Xena   o**X**

Writing "W·w / X·x"

■ Trace and then write each letter while saying it aloud.

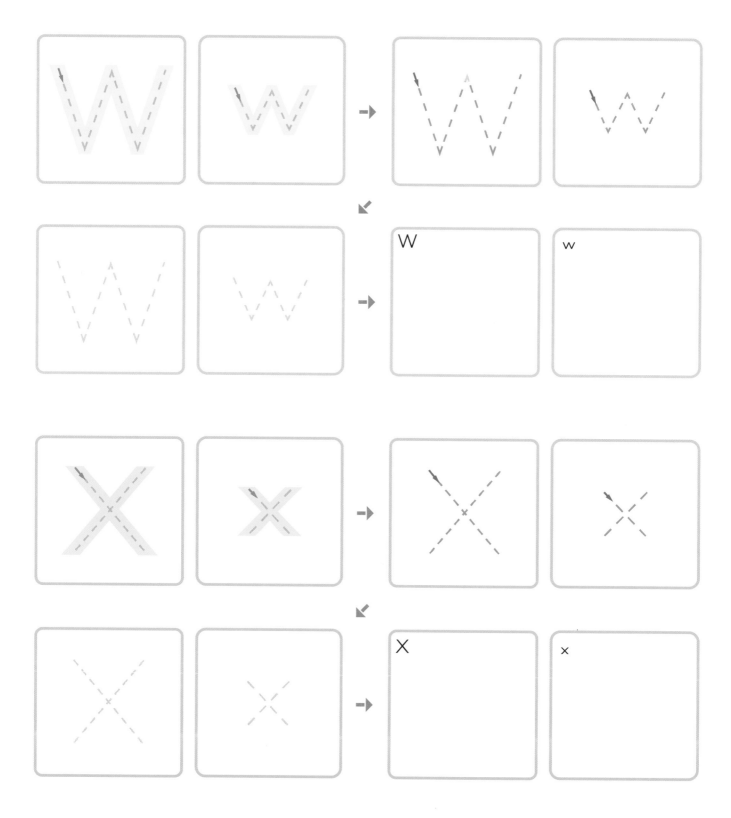

■ Trace each letter while saying it aloud.

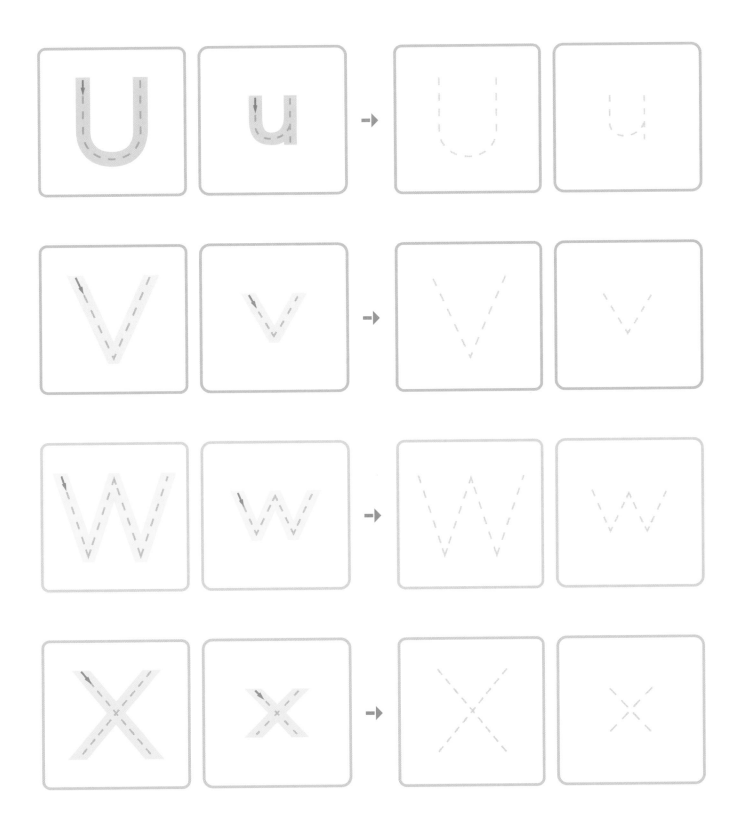

Writing "U·u → X·x"

■ Trace and then write each letter while saying it aloud.

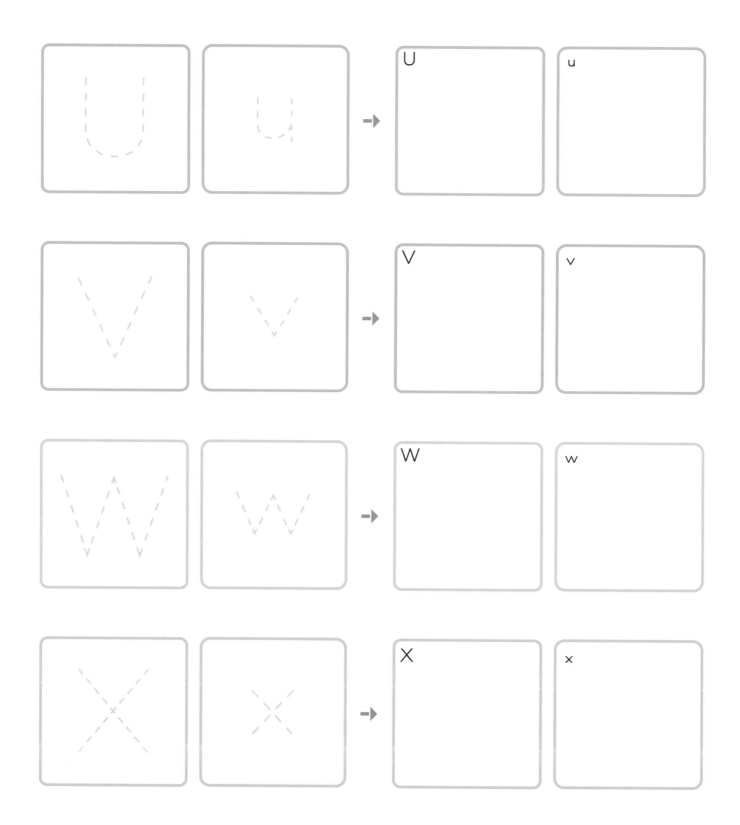

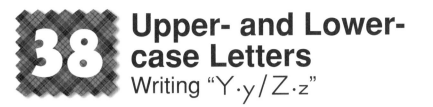

Upper- and Lower-case Letters
Writing "Y·y / Z·z"

Name

Date

■ Look at the first letters of the words below. Then trace the letters.

Yan   yak   Yan   Yak

Zeb   zebra   Zeb   Zebra

Writing "Y·y / Z·z"

■ Trace and then write each letter while saying it aloud.

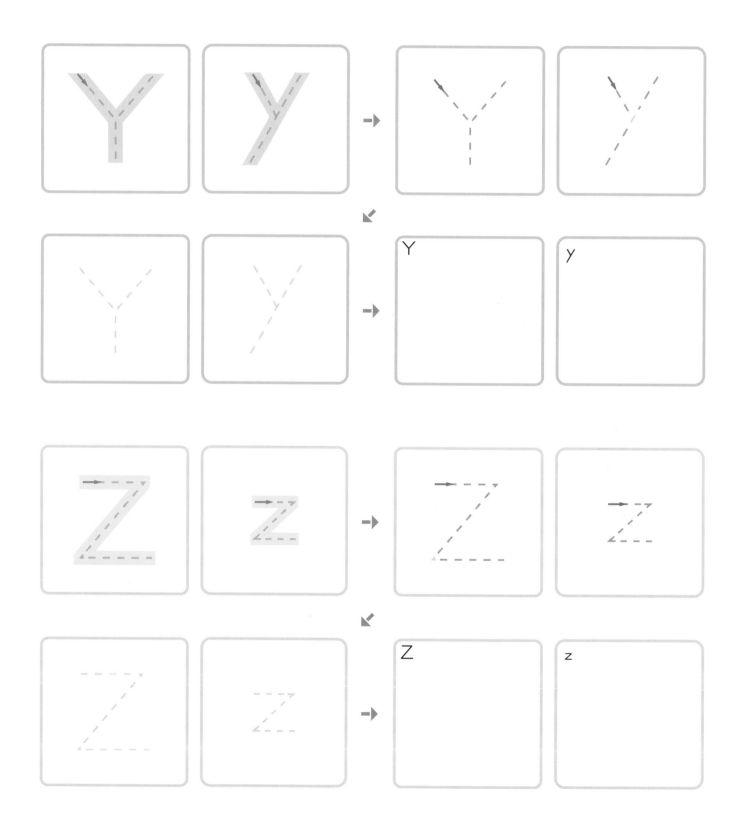

■ Trace each letter while saying it aloud.

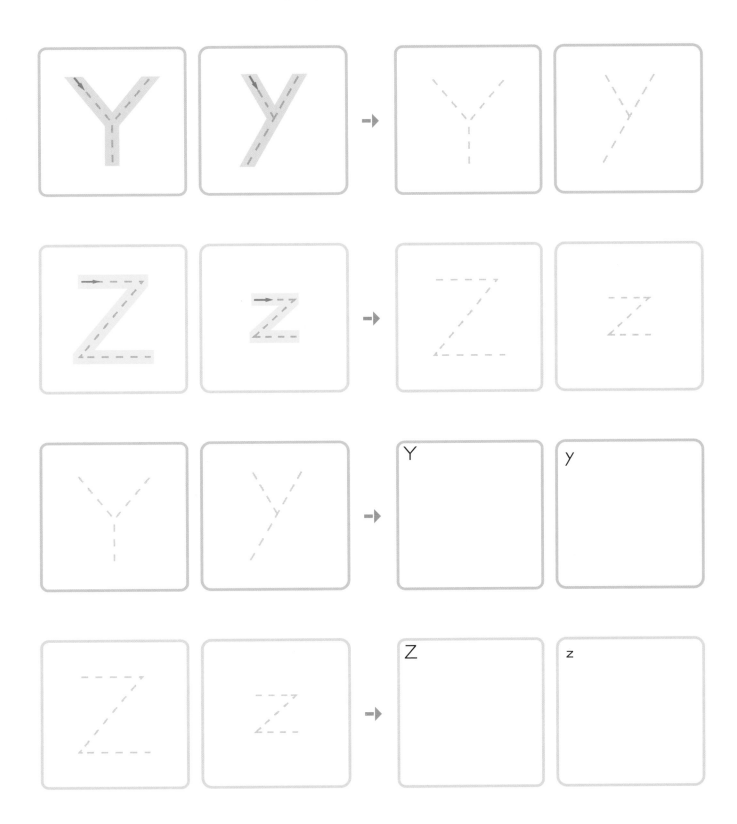

Writing "A·a → I·i"

■ Write each letter while saying it aloud.

A	a	B	b
C	c	D	d
E	e	F	f
G	g	H	h
I	i		

Name

Date

■ Write each letter while saying it aloud.

J	j	K	k
L	l	M	m
N	n	O	o
P	p	Q	q
R	r		

Writing "S·s → Z·z"

To parents
Your child has been developing his or her understanding of alphabetical order and letter formation, which are necessary for future verbal skills. Please encourage your child and nurture a lifelong love of reading and writing.

■ Write each letter while saying it aloud.

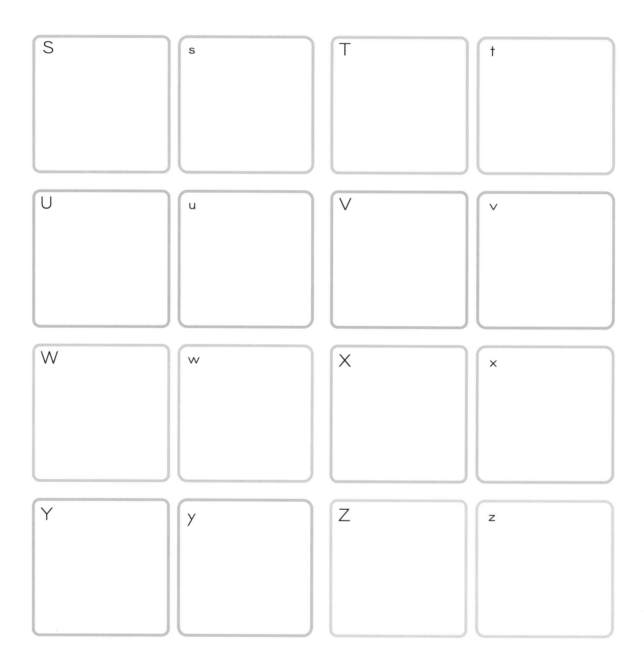

S | s | T | t

U | u | V | v

W | w | X | x

Y | y | Z | z

My Big Book of NUMBERS, LETTERS & WORDS

RHYMING WORDS

Table of Contents

To parents: RHYMING WORDS

In this section, your child will continue to develop his or her ability to understand letter sounds. Your child will learn how to blend letter sounds together to say and write short rhyming words. The section will begin by reviewing the alphabet and gradually move to have your child recite and write rhyming words. Through simple entertaining exercises and mazes, this section will increase your child's ability to recognize and write words in an easy and enjoyable way.

Each topic is presented in Kumon's step-by-step method to allow your child to learn verbal skills without frustration. Your child will be able to learn new words naturally by writing letters in familiar words and saying those words again and again. This will help your child build confidence that will help him or her begin a lifelong journey of reading.

The activities in this section will help your child build a foundation for future reading and writing skills. If your child is ready to advance to the next skill after completing this section, please refer to the appropriate book from our other Verbal Skills products for further work.

My Book of RHYMING WORDS & PHRASES

My Book of RHYMING WORDS LONG VOWELS

How to hold a pencil properly

There are several ways to teach children to hold a pencil properly. Here is one example.

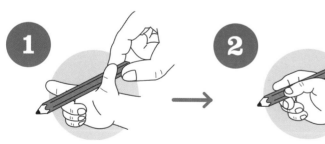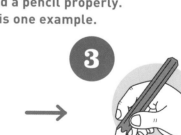

1 Help your child form an "L" shape with his or her thumb and forefinger as pictured here. Place the pencil against the top of the bent middle finger and on the thumb joint.

2 Now, have your child squeeze the pencil with the thumb and forefinger.

3 Check the way that your child is holding the pencil against the picture to decide whether or not it is the proper way.

It can be difficult for a child who does not yet have enough strength in his or her hand and fingers to hold the pencil properly. Please teach this skill gradually, so that your child will remaln interested and willing to hold a pencil naturally.

Review of Alphabet
Writing a-z

Name

Date

To parents
Guide your child to write his or her name and date in the box above. On pages 167 and 168, your child will review the letters of the alphabet. Please help your child as needed and praise him or her at the completion of each exercise.

■ Trace the letters a to z.

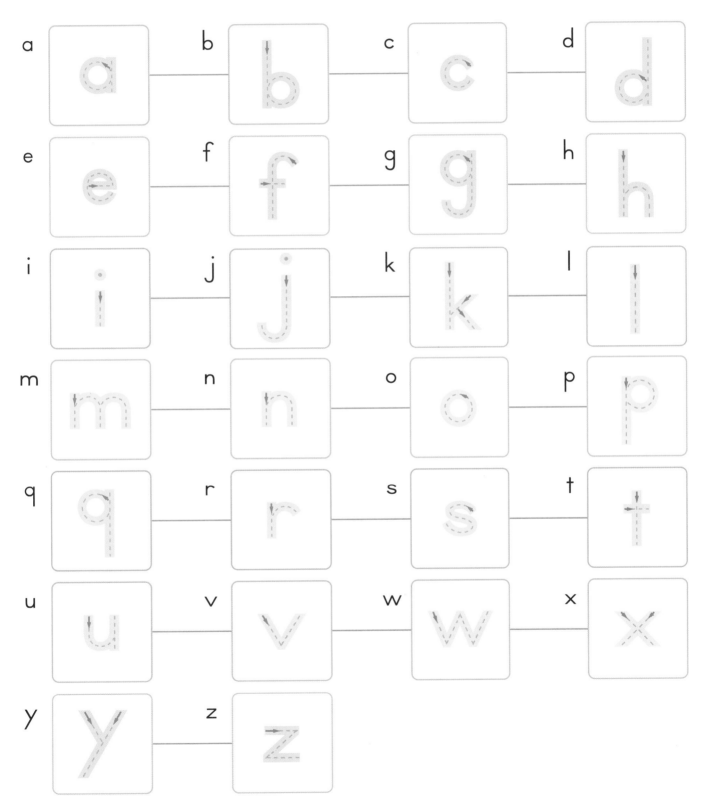

a   b   c   d

e   f   g   h

i   j   k   l

m   n   o   p

q   r   s   t

u   v   w   x

y   z

Writing a-z

■ Trace the letters a to z.

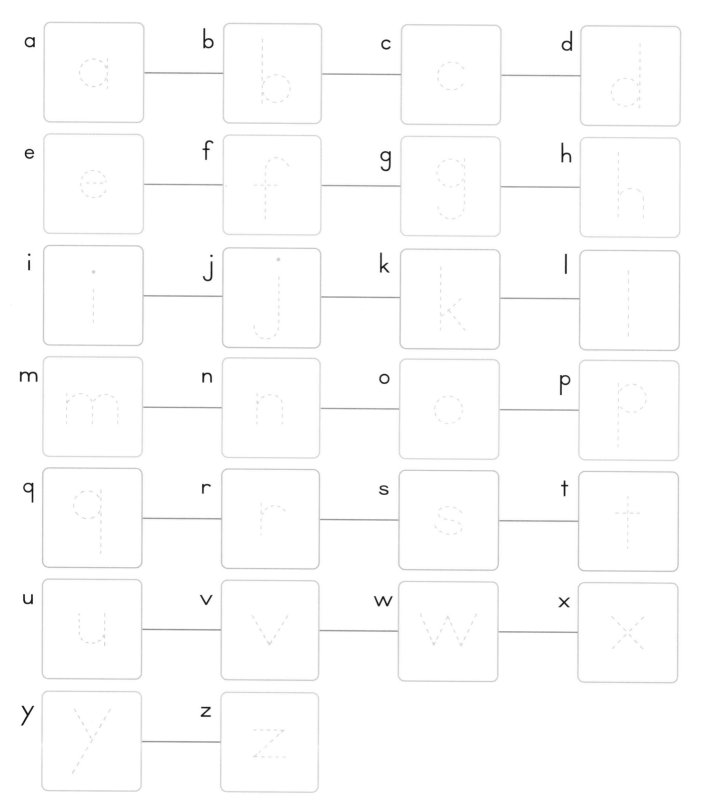

2 What Is It?

Saying "_at" Sounds

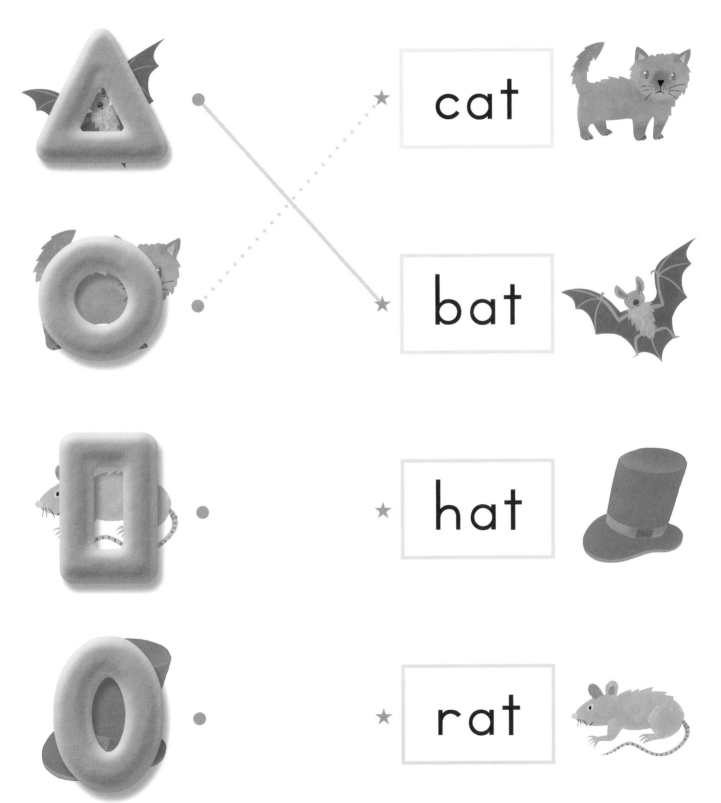

Name

Date

To parents
By repeating rhyming words with the short "a" vowel sound, your child will gain an awareness of the connection between letters and the sounds they represent. Give your child plenty of encouragement and praise your child at the completion of each exercise.

■ Match the pictures by drawing a line from the dot (●) to the star (★).

cat

bat

hat

rat

169

Saying "_at" Sounds

■ Draw a line from the dot (●) to the star (★) while saying each word.

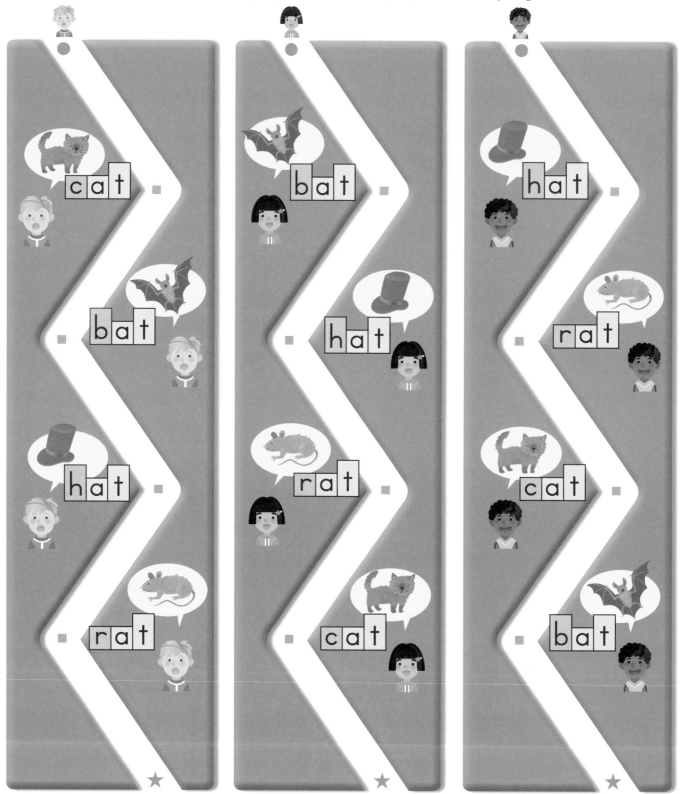

Rhyming Words

Writing "_at" Words

To parents

Please help your child to say the sound of the individual letters as he or she traces them. Children should not be forced to blend the letters together or to try sounding out the words. If children are allowed to demonstrate their skills naturally, after they have had sufficient practice, then they will have more positive feelings about independent learning.

■ Say the word. Then say the sound of each letter as you trace it.

Writing "_at" Words

■ Say the word. Then say the sound of each letter as you trace and write it.

cat

bat

hat

rat

What Is It?

Saying "_an" Sounds

Date

■ Match the pictures by drawing a line from the dot (●) to the star (★).

173

Saying "_an" Sounds

■ Draw a line from the dot (●) to the star (★) while saying each word.

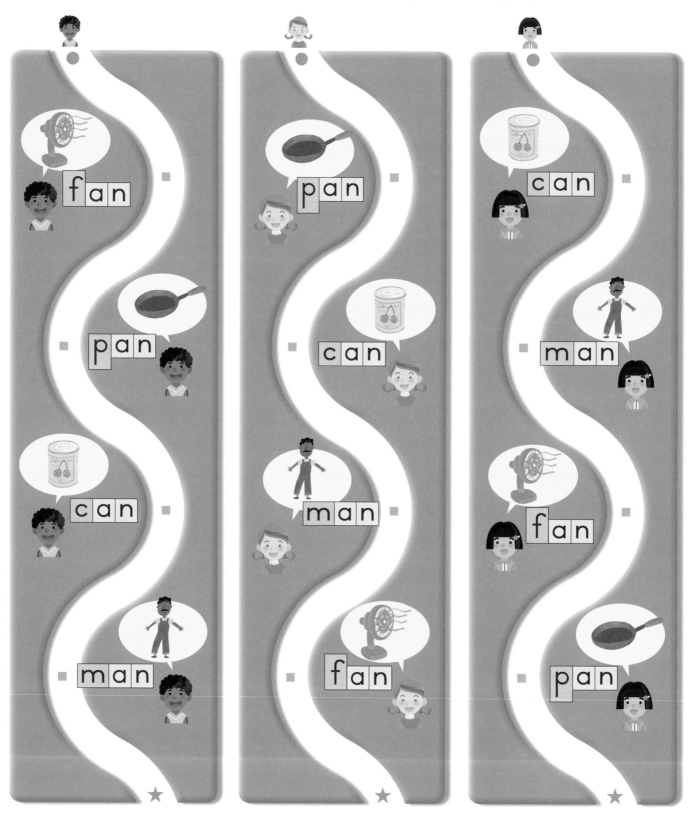

■ Say the word. Then say the sound of each letter as you trace it.

fan

pan

can

man

Writing "_an" Words

■ Say the word. Then say the sound of each letter as you trace and write it.

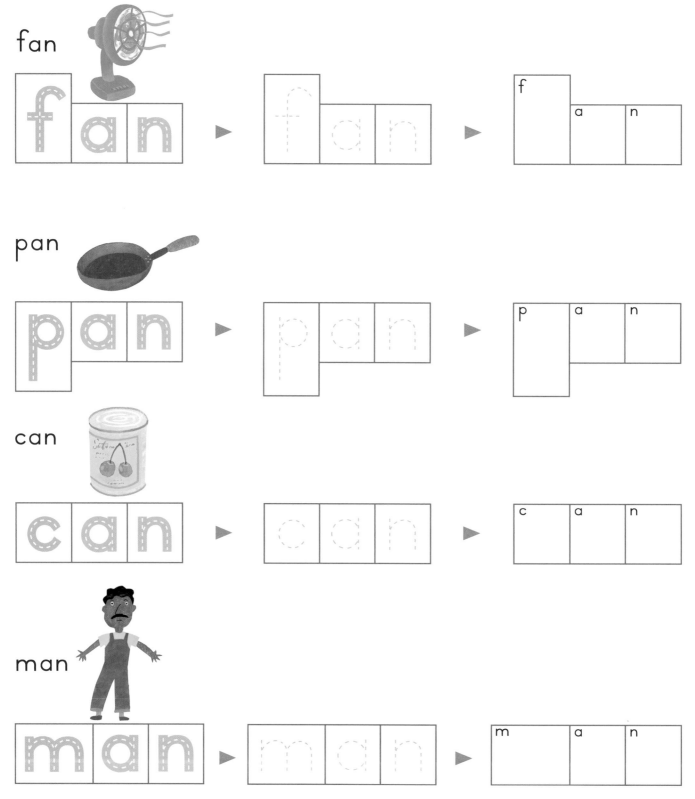

fan

pan

can

man

What Is It?

Saying "_ap" Sounds

Name

Date

■ Match the pictures by drawing a line from the dot (●) to the star (★).

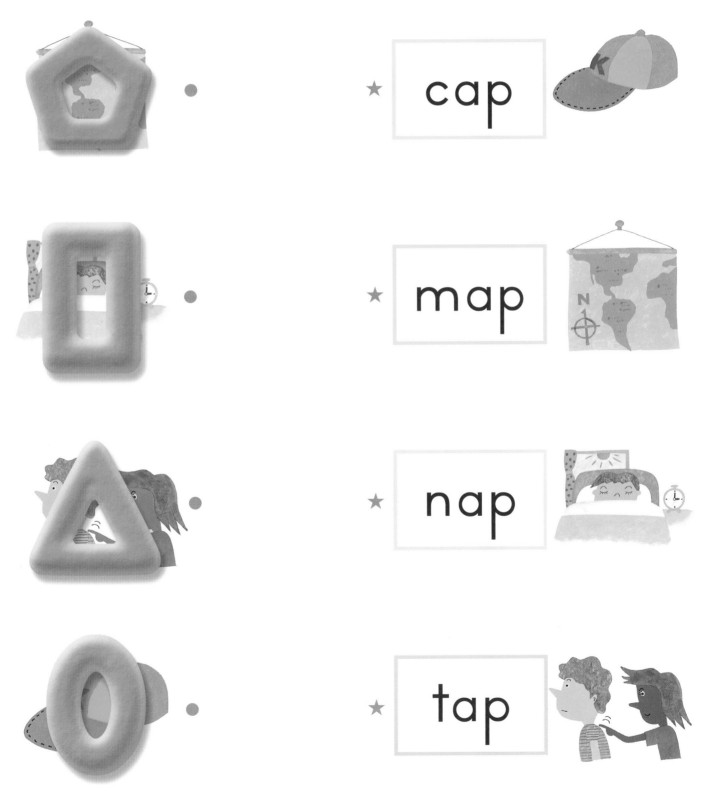

★ cap

★ map

★ nap

★ tap

177

Saying "_ap" Sounds

■ Draw a line from the dot (●) to the star (★) while saying each word.

Rhyming Words

Writing "_ap" Words

■ Say the word. Then say the sound of each letter as you trace it.

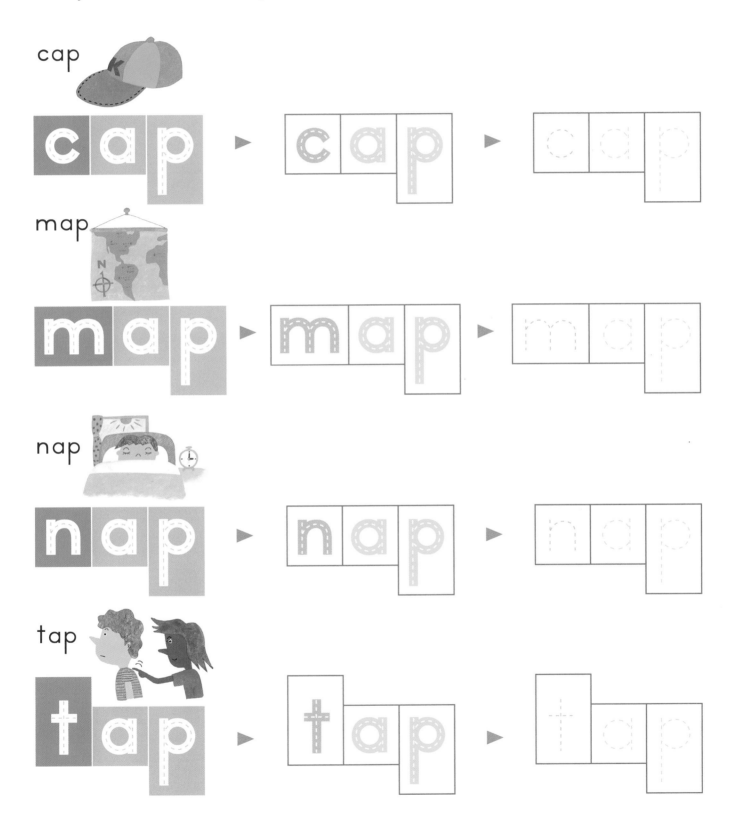

cap

map

nap

tap

Writing "_ap" Words

■ Say the word. Then say the sound of each letter as you trace and write it.

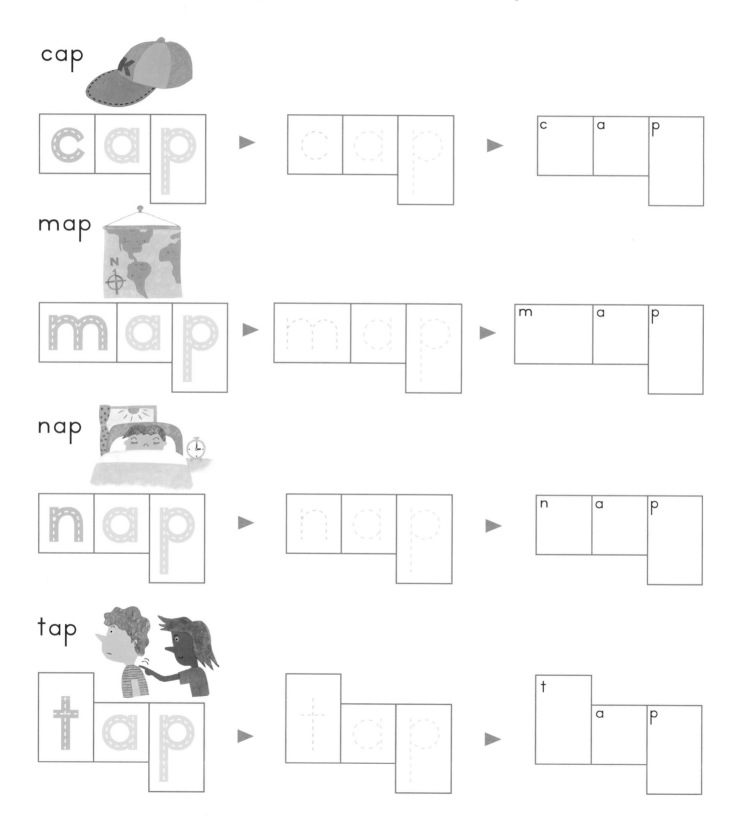

cap

map

nap

tap

What Is It?

Saying "_ad" Sounds

Name

Date

■ Match the pictures by drawing a line from the dot (●) to the star (★).

dad

sad

pad

lad

181

Saying "_ad" Sounds

■ Draw a line from the dot (●) to the star (★) while saying each word.

Name
Date

■ Say the word. Then say the sound of each letter as you trace it.

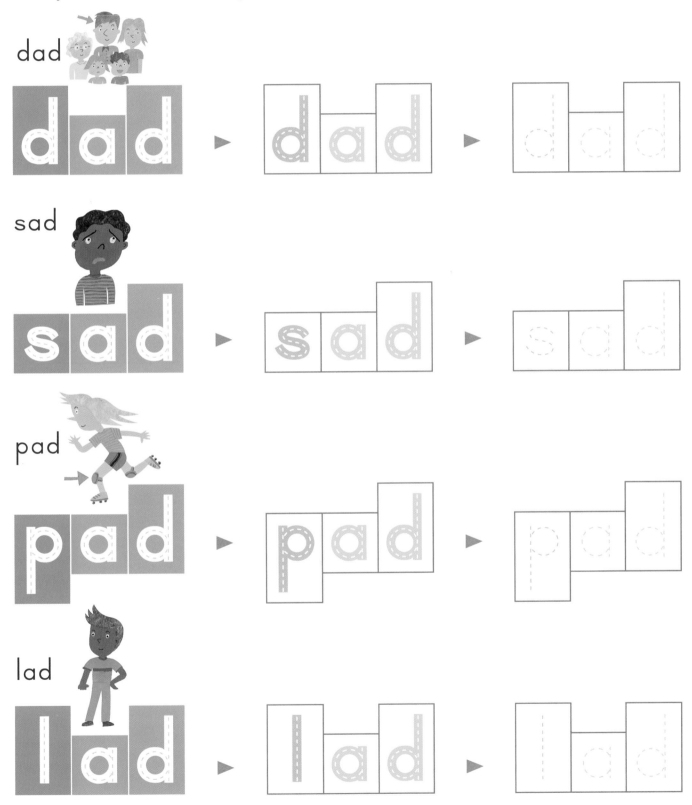

dad

sad

pad

lad

183

Writing "_ad" Words

■ Say the word. Then say the sound of each letter as you trace and write it.

dad

d a d ▸ d a d ▸ d a d

sad

s a d ▸ s a d ▸ s a d

pad

p a d ▸ p a d ▸ p a d

lad

l a d ▸ l a d ▸ l a d

Review

Saying "_at" and "_an" Words

Name

Date

- Draw a line from 🧒 to 🧒 while saying each "_at" word.
  Draw a line from 👧 to 👧 while saying each "_an" word.

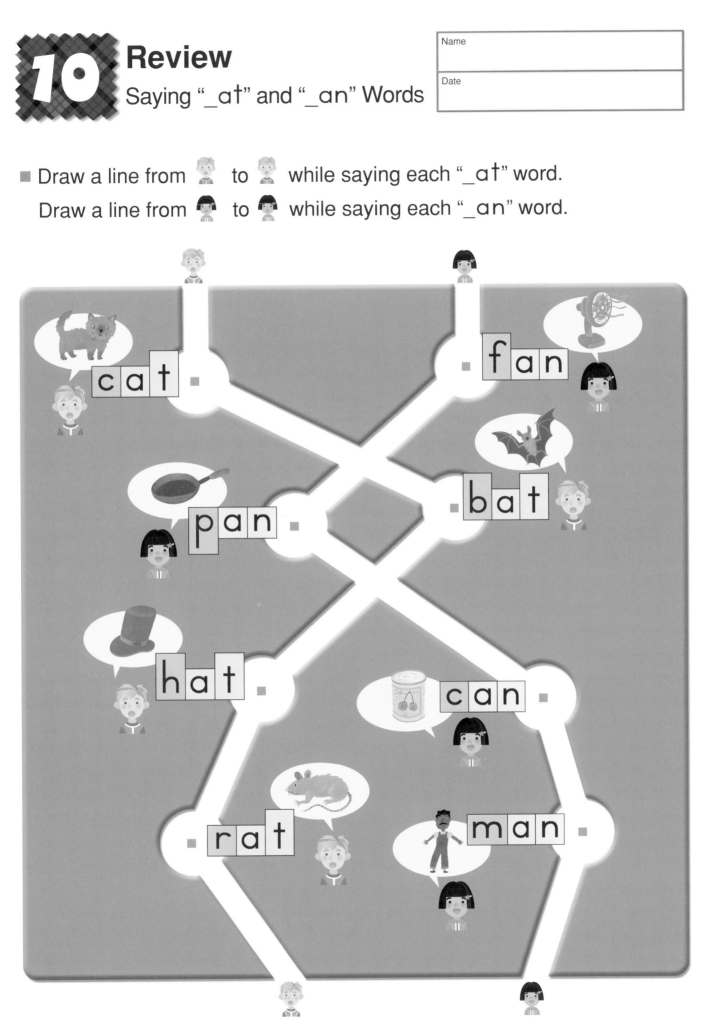

Writing "_at" and "_an" Words

■ Say the word. Then say the sound of each letter as you write it.

cat

| c | a | t |

fan

| f | a | n |

bat

| b | a | t |

pan

| p | a | n |

hat

| h | a | t |

can

| c | a | n |

rat

| r | a | t |

man

| m | a | n |

■ Draw a line from 🧒 to 🧒 while saying each "_ap" word.
Draw a line from 👧 to 👧 while saying each "_ad" word.

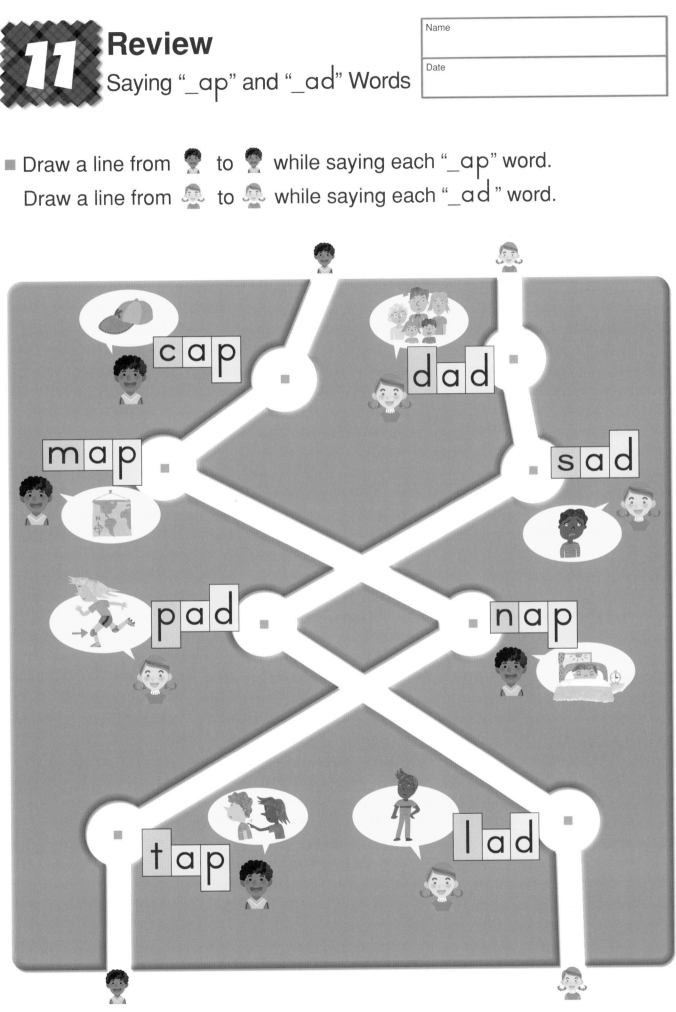

Writing "_ap" and "_ad" Words

■ Say the word. Then say the sound of each letter as you write it.

cap

| c | a | p |

dad

| d | a | d |

map

| m | a | p |

sad

| s | a | d |

nap

| n | a | p |

pad

| p | a | d |

tap

| t | a | p |

lad

| l | a | d |

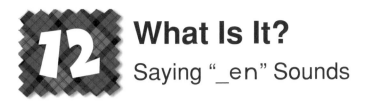
| Name |
| Date |

To parents
By repeating rhyming words with the short "e" vowel sound, your child will gain an awareness of the connection between letters and the sounds they represent.

■ Match the pictures by drawing a line from the dot (●) to the star (★).

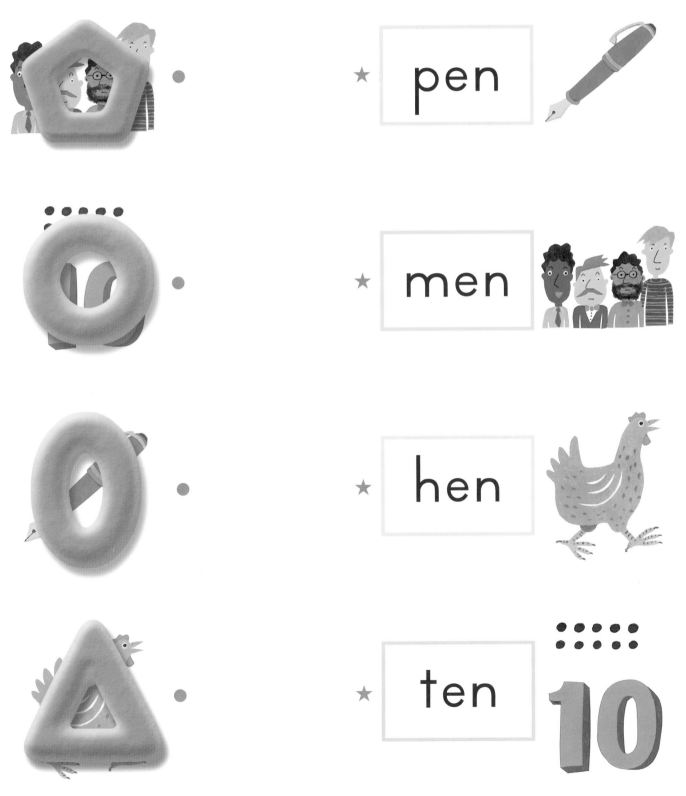

Saying "_en" Sounds

■ Draw a line from the dot (●) to the star (★) while saying each word.

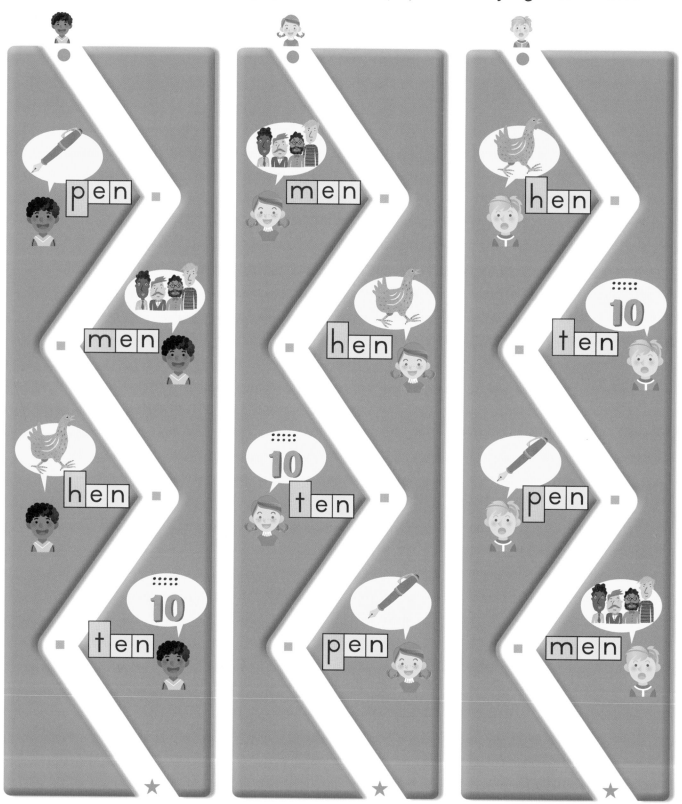

Rhyming Words

Writing "_en" Words

■ Say the word. Then say the sound of each letter as you trace it.

pen

men

hen

ten

Writing "_en" Words

■ Say the word. Then say the sound of each letter as you trace and write it.

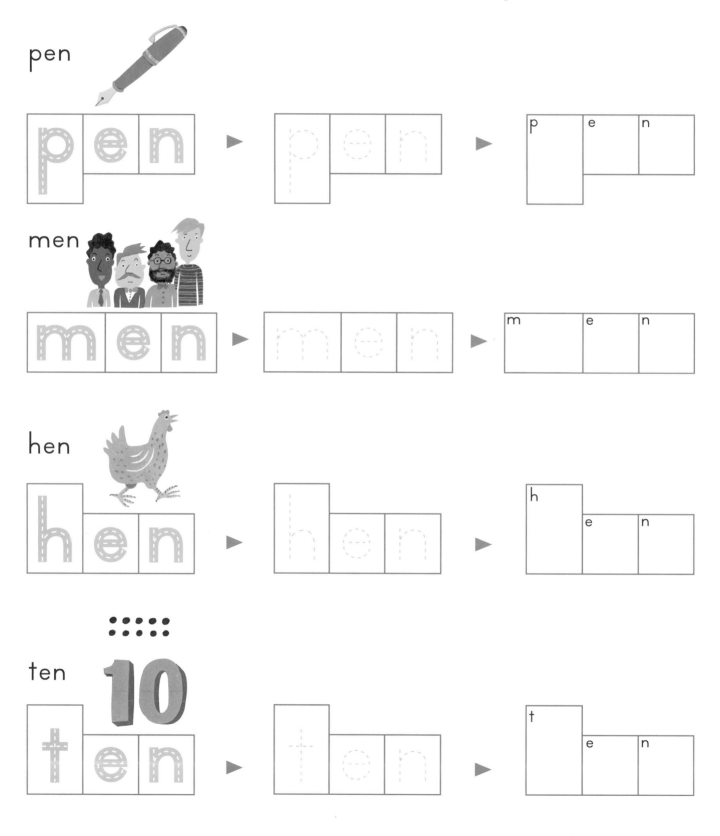

pen

men

hen

ten

What Is It?

Saying "_et" Sounds

■ Match the pictures by drawing a line from the dot (●) to the star (★).

★ net

★ wet

★ pet

★ get

193

Saying "_et" Sounds

■ Draw a line from the dot (●) to the star (★) while saying each word.

Rhyming Words

Writing "_et" Words

Name

Date

■ Say the word. Then say the sound of each letter as you trace it.

net

wet

pet

get

Writing "_et" Words

■ Say the word. Then say the sound of each letter as you trace and write it.

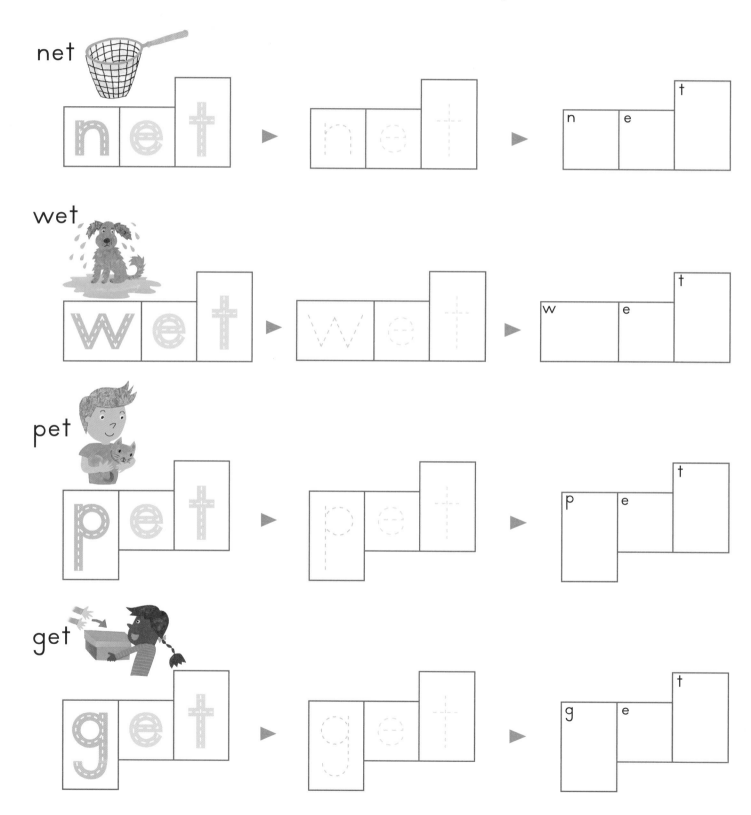

net

wet

pet

get

Name

Date

■ Draw a line from 🧑 to 🧑 while saying each "_en" word.
Draw a line from 👧 to 👧 while saying each "_et" word.

Writing "_en" and "_et" Words

■ Say the word. Then say the sound of each letter as you write it.

pen

| p | e | n |

net

| n | e | t |

men

| m | e | n |

wet

| w | e | t |

hen

| h | | |
| | e | n |

pet

| p | e | t |

ten

| t | | |
| | e | n |

get

| g | e | t |

17 What Is It?

Saying "_ig" Sounds

Name

Date

To parents
By repeating rhyming words, your child will gain an awareness of the connection between letters and the sounds they represent.

■ Match the pictures by drawing a line from the dot (●) to the star (★).

★ pig

★ wig

★ dig

★ big

Saying "_ig" Sounds

■ Draw a line from the dot (●) to the star (★) while saying each word.

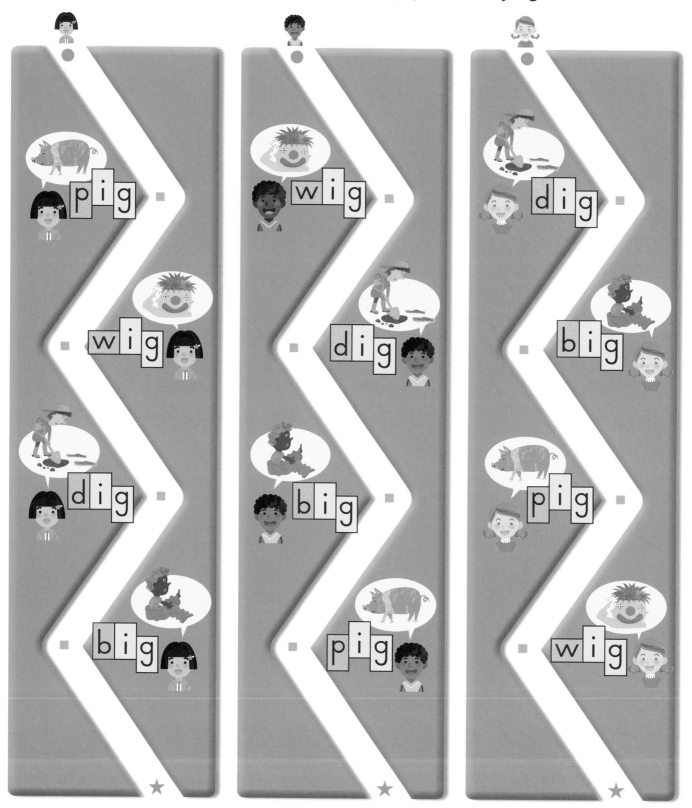

18 Rhyming Words
Writing "_ig" Words

Name
Date

■ Say the word. Then say the sound of each letter as you trace it.

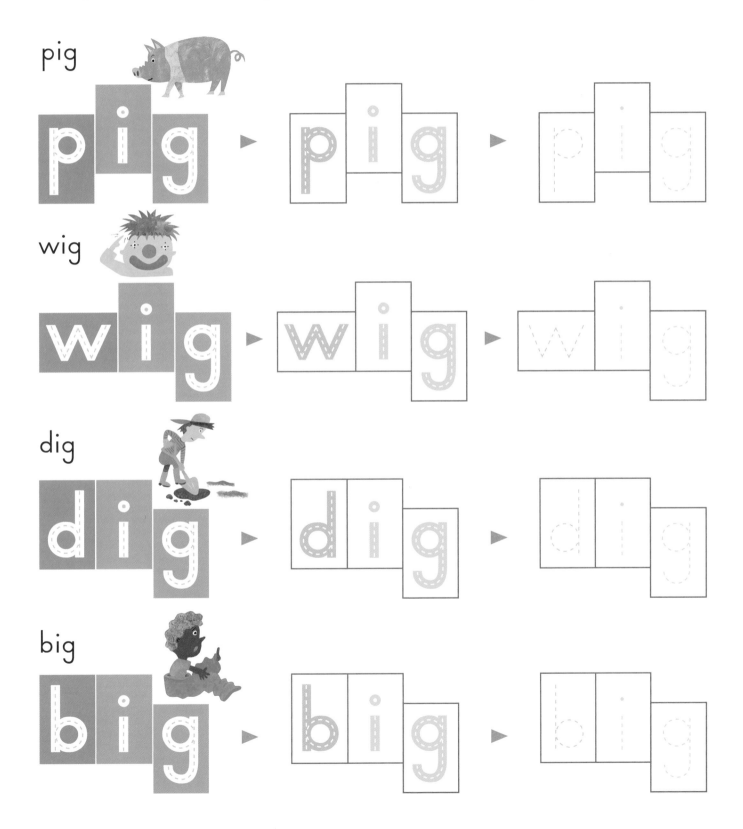

pig

wig

dig

big

Writing "_ig" Words

■ Say the word. Then say the sound of each letter as you trace and write it.

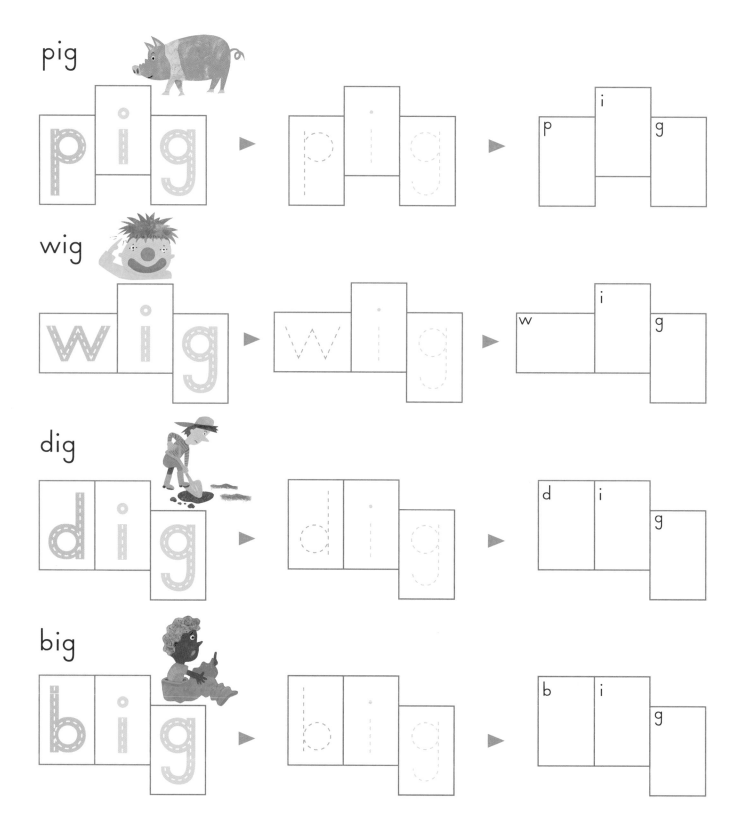

pig

wig

dig

big

What Is It?

Saying "_in" Sounds

■ Match the pictures by drawing a line from the dot (●) to the star (★).

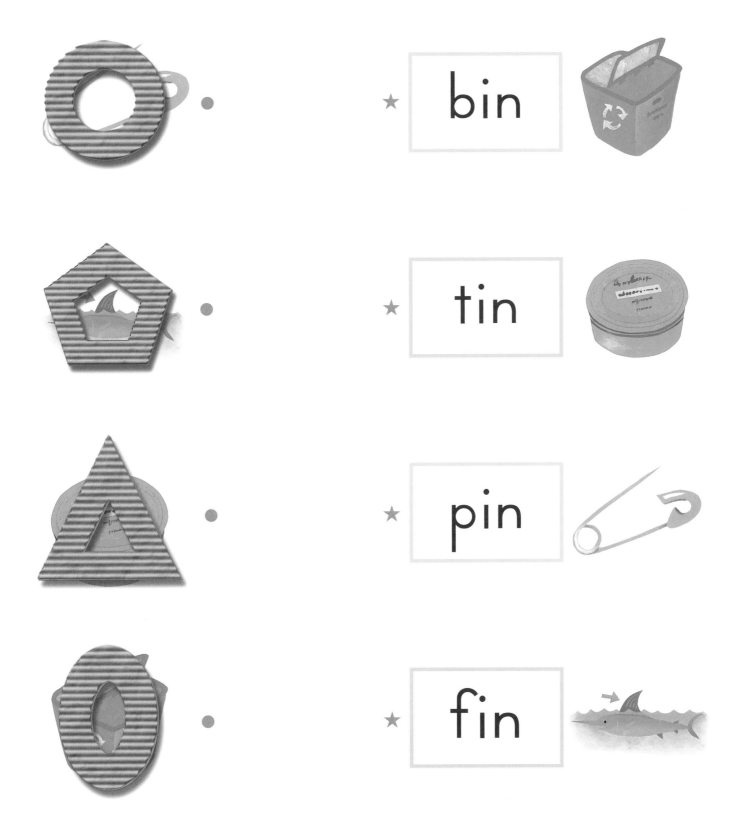

★ bin

★ tin

★ pin

★ fin

Saying "_in" Sounds

■ Draw a line from the dot (●) to the star (★) while saying each word.

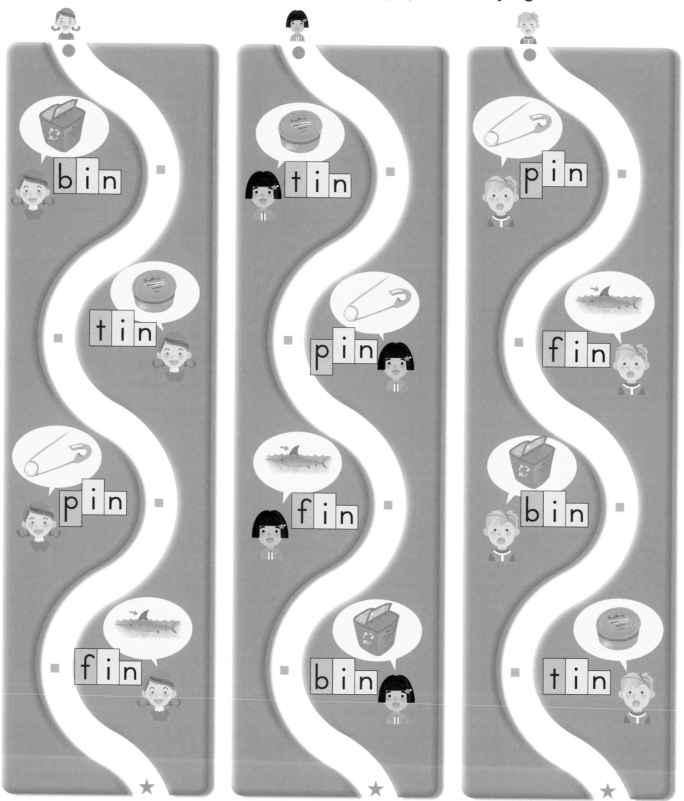

Rhyming Words

Writing "_in" Words

Name

Date

■ Say the word. Then say the sound of each letter as you trace it.

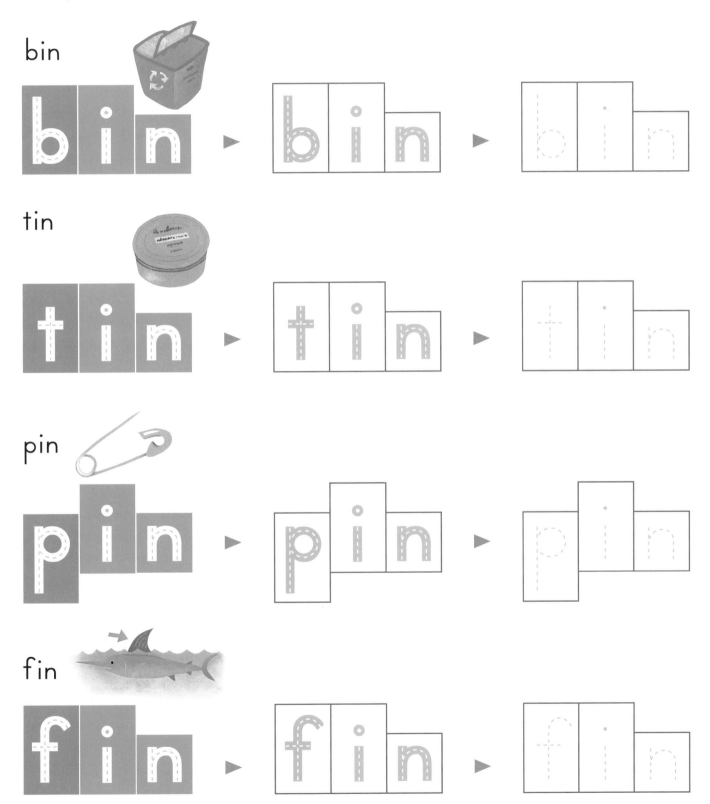

bin

tin

pin

fin

Writing "_in" Words

■ Say the word. Then say the sound of each letter as you trace and write it.

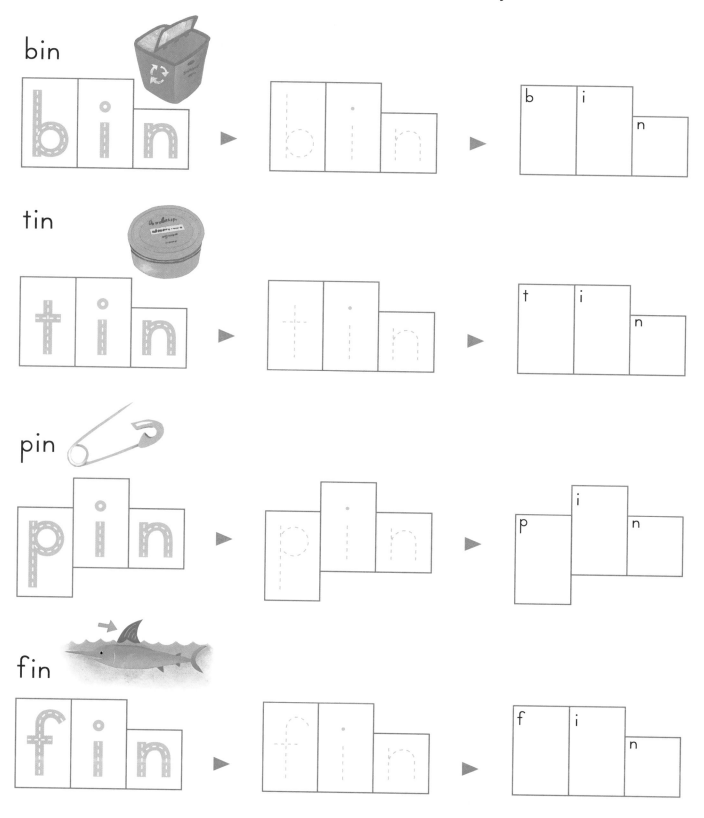

bin

tin

pin

fin

21 What Is It?

Saying "_ip" Sounds

Name

Date

■ Match the pictures by drawing a line from the dot (●) to the star (★).

★ hip

★ lip

★ zip

★ rip

Saying "_ip" Sounds

■ Draw a line from the dot (●) to the star (★) while saying each word.

22 Rhyming Words

Writing "_ip" Words

Name

Date

■ Say the word. Then say the sound of each letter as you trace it.

hip

lip

zip

rip

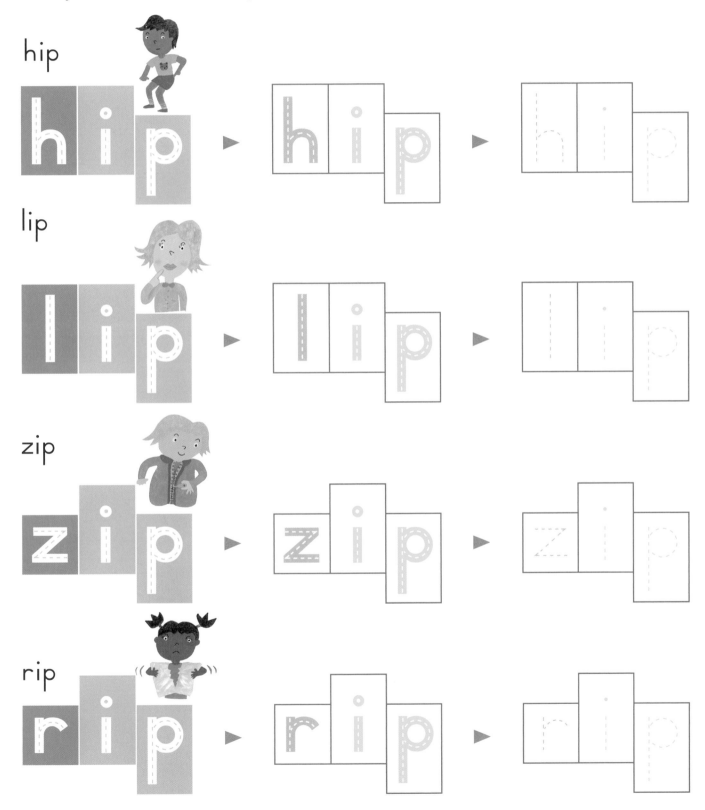

Writing "_ip" Words

■ Say the word. Then say the sound of each letter as you trace and write it.

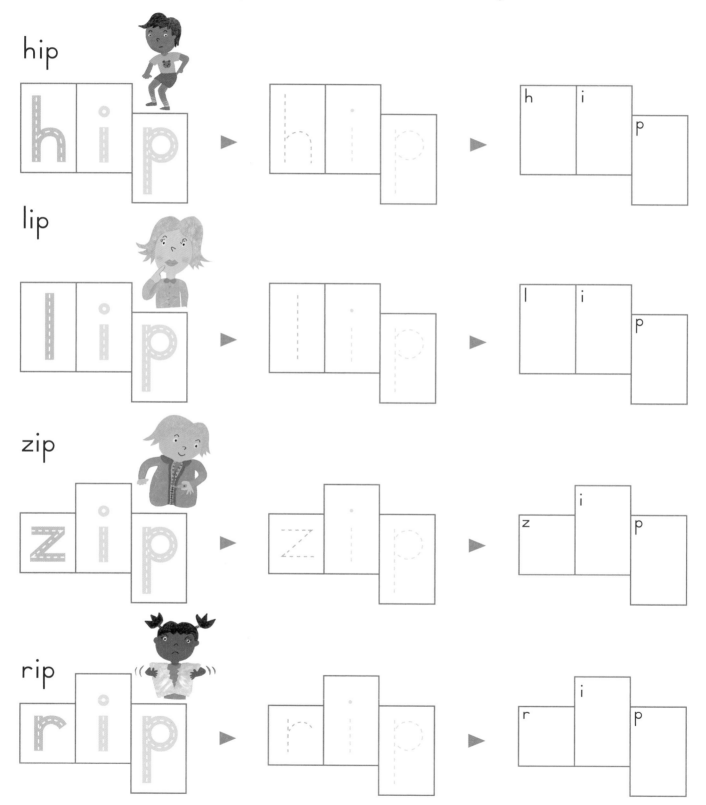

hip

lip

zip

rip

Review

Saying "_ig" and "_in" Words

■ Draw a line from to while saying each "_ig" word.
Draw a line from to while saying each "_in" word.

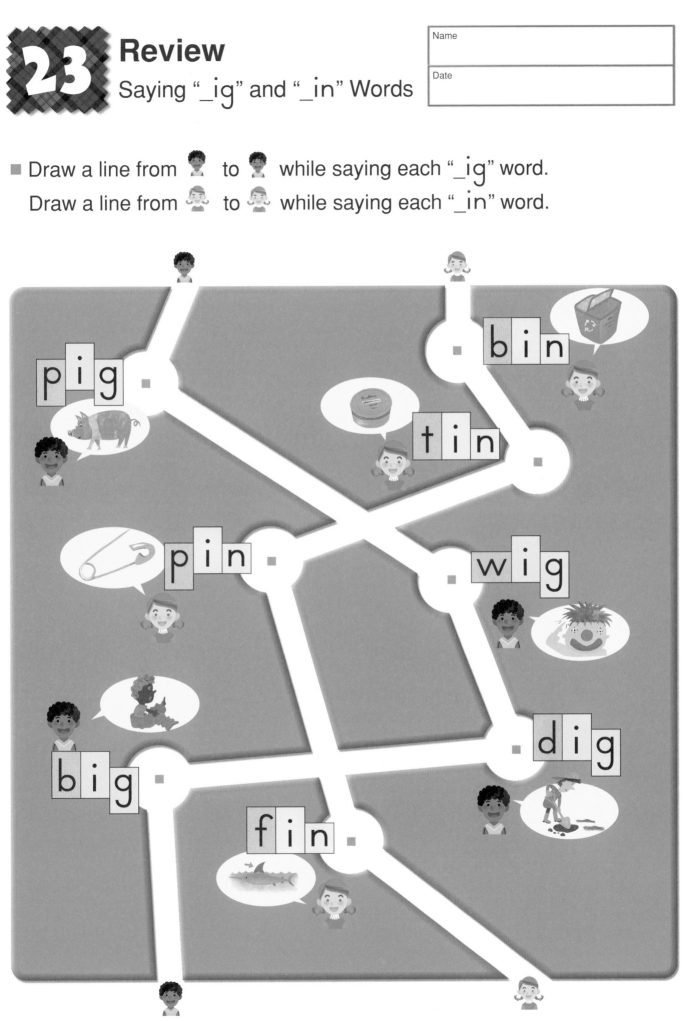

Writing "_ig" and "_in" Words

■ Say the word. Then say the sound of each letter as you write it.

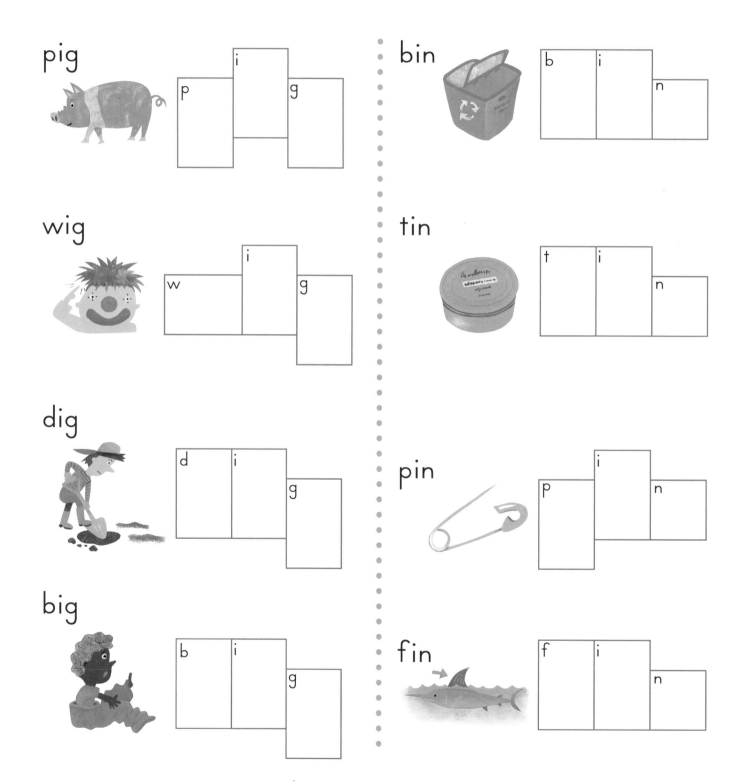

pig

| p | i | g |

wig

| w | i | g |

dig

| d | i | g |

big

| b | i | g |

bin

| b | i | n |

tin

| t | i | n |

pin

| p | i | n |

fin

| f | i | n |

■ Draw a line from 👦 to 👦 while saying each "_ip" word.
Draw a line from 👧 to 👧 while saying each "_ig" word.

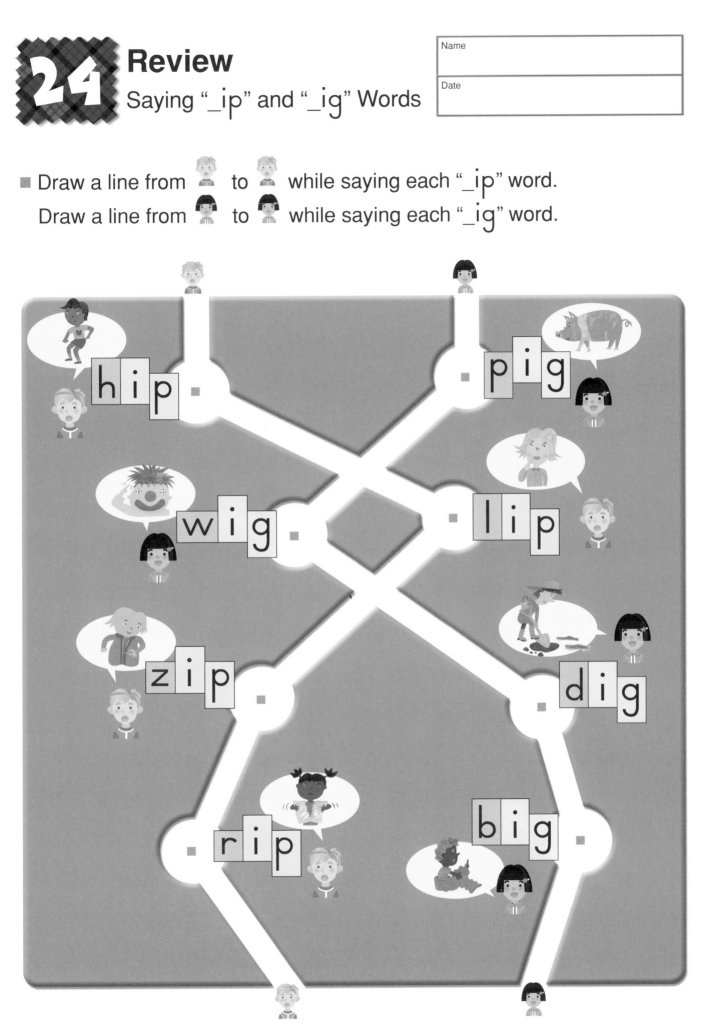

Writing "_ip" and "_ig" Words

■ Say the word. Then say the sound of each letter as you write it.

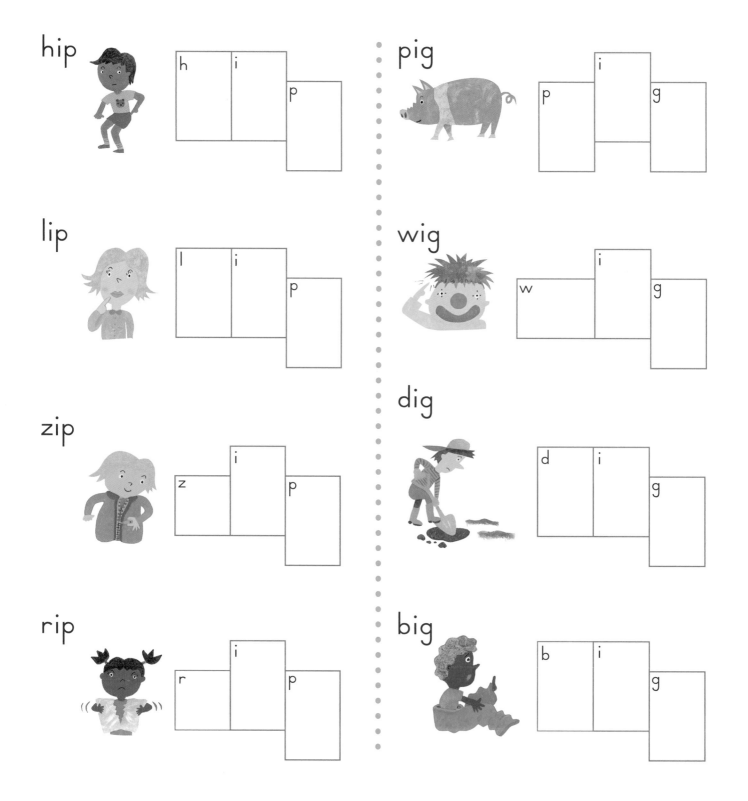

hip

| h | i | |
| | | p |

pig

| | i | |
| p | | g |

lip

| l | i | |
| | | p |

wig

| | i | |
| w | | g |

zip

| | i | |
| z | | p |

dig

| d | i | |
| | | g |

rip

| | i | |
| r | | p |

big

| b | i | |
| | | g |

What Is It?

Saying "_op" Sounds

■ Match the pictures by drawing a line from the dot (●) to the star (★).

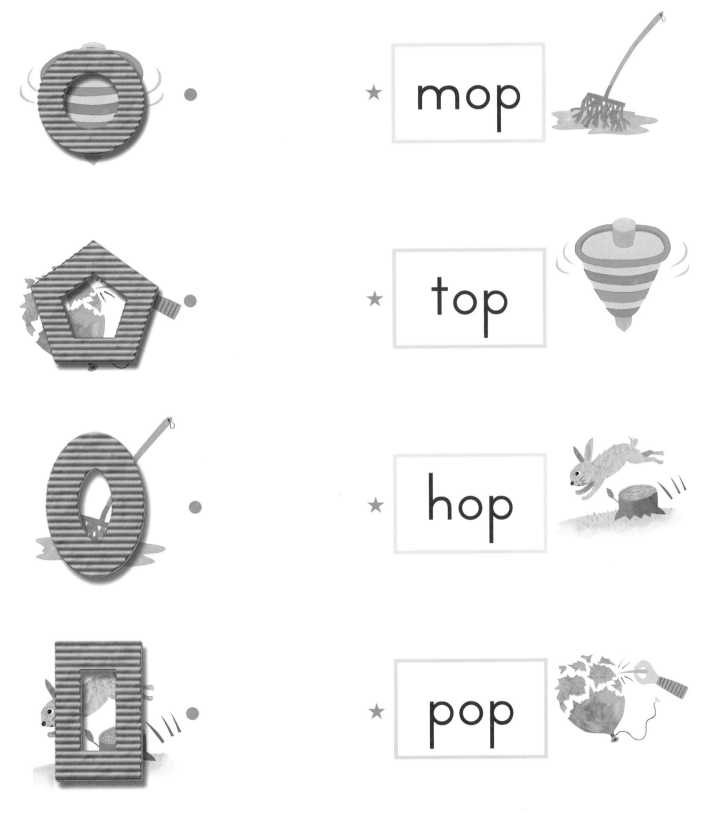

mop

top

hop

pop

Saying "_op" Sounds

■ Draw a line from the dot (●) to the star (★) while saying each word.

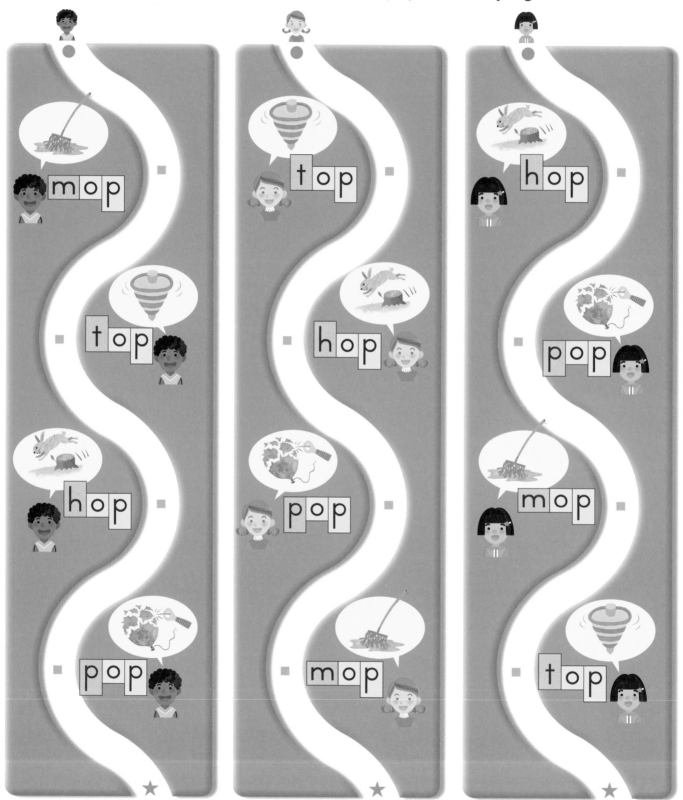

Rhyming Words
Writing "_op" Words

Name

Date

■ Say the word. Then say the sound of each letter as you trace it.

mop

top

hop

pop

217

Writing "_op" Words

■ Say the word. Then say the sound of each letter as you trace and write it.

mop

top

hop

pop

■ Match the pictures by drawing a line from the dot (●) to the star (★).

★ dog

★ log

★ hog

★ jog

Saying "_og" Sounds

■ Draw a line from the dot (●) to the star (★) while saying each word.

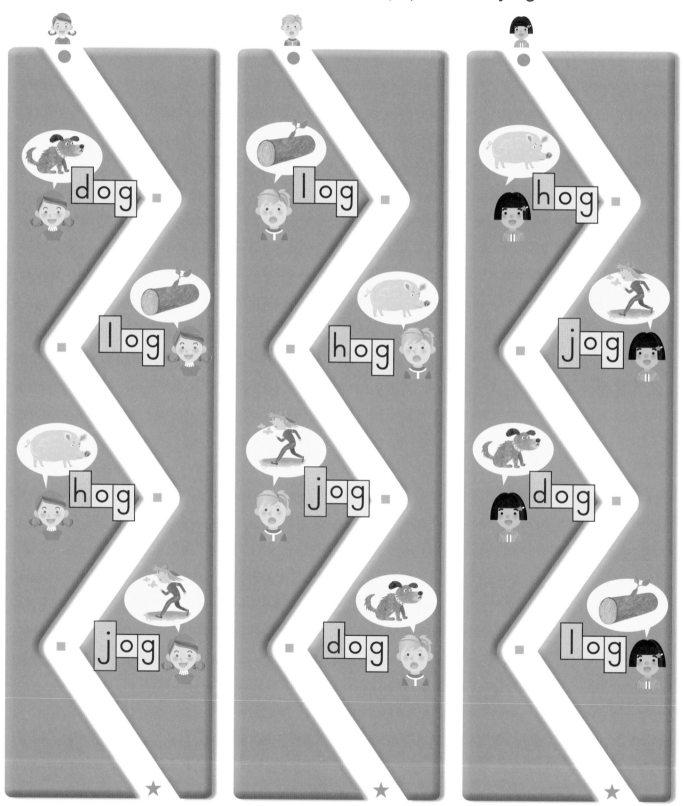

Rhyming Words

Writing "_og" Words

Name

Date

■ Say the word. Then say the sound of each letter as you trace it.

dog

log

hog

jog

Writing "_og" Words

■ Say the word. Then say the sound of each letter as you trace and write it.

dog

log

hog

jog

29 **Review**

Saying "_op" and "_og" Words

Name

Date

■ Draw a line from 🧒 to 🧒 while saying each "_op" word.
Draw a line from 👧 to 👧 while saying each "_og" word.

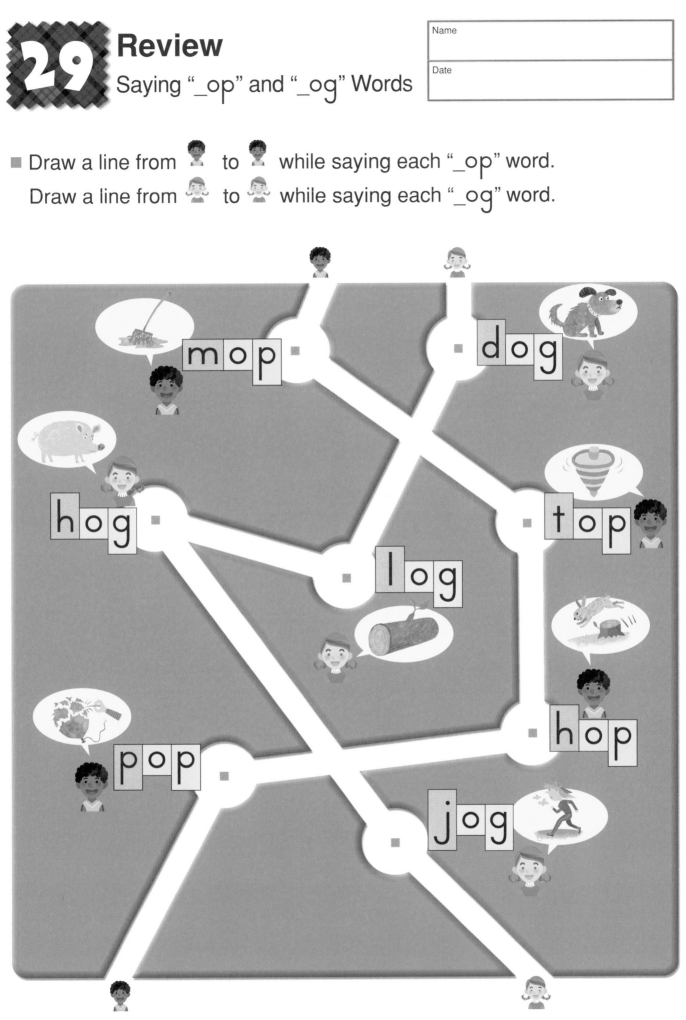

223

Writing "_op" and "_og" Words

■ Say the word. Then say the sound of each letter as you write it.

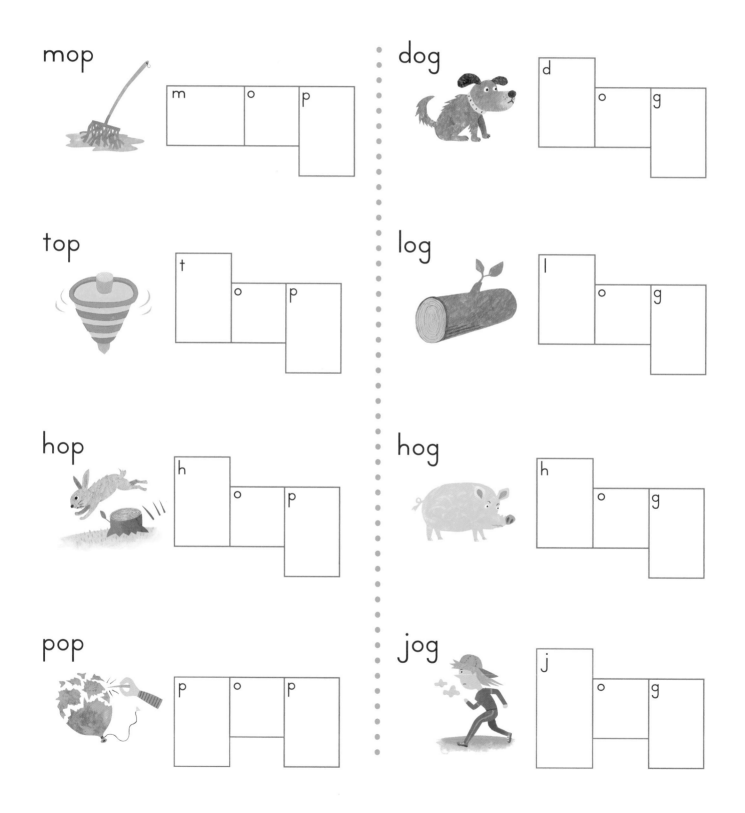

mop

| m | o | p |

top

| t | o | p |

hop

| h | o | p |

pop

| p | o | p |

dog

| d | o | g |

log

| l | o | g |

hog

| h | o | g |

jog

| j | o | g |

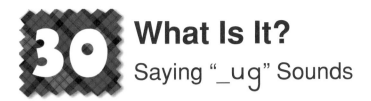
■ Match the pictures by drawing a line from the dot (●) to the star (★).

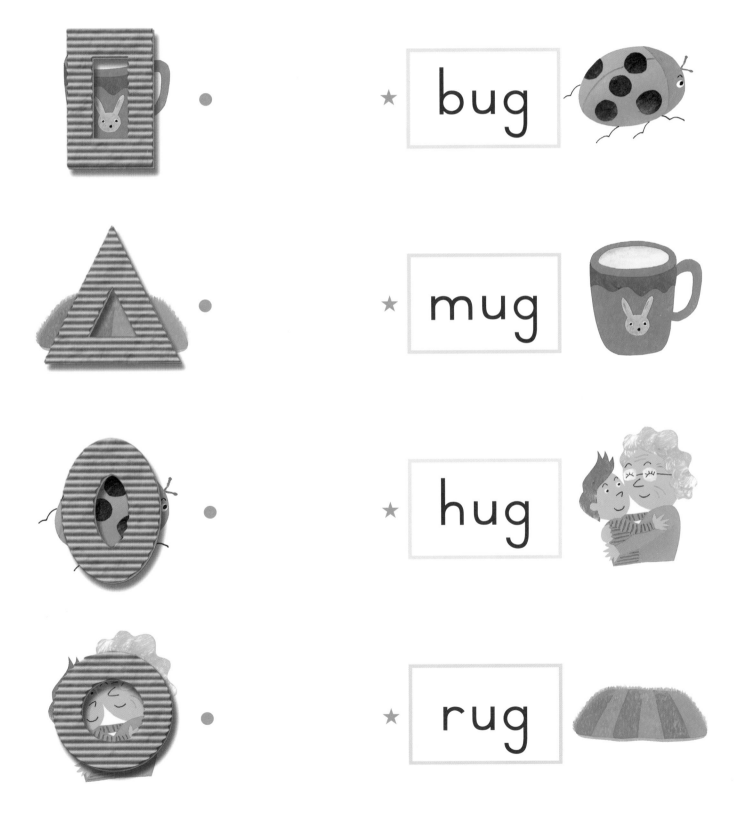

★ bug

★ mug

★ hug

★ rug

Saying "_ug" Sounds

■ Draw a line from the dot (●) to the star (★) while saying each word.

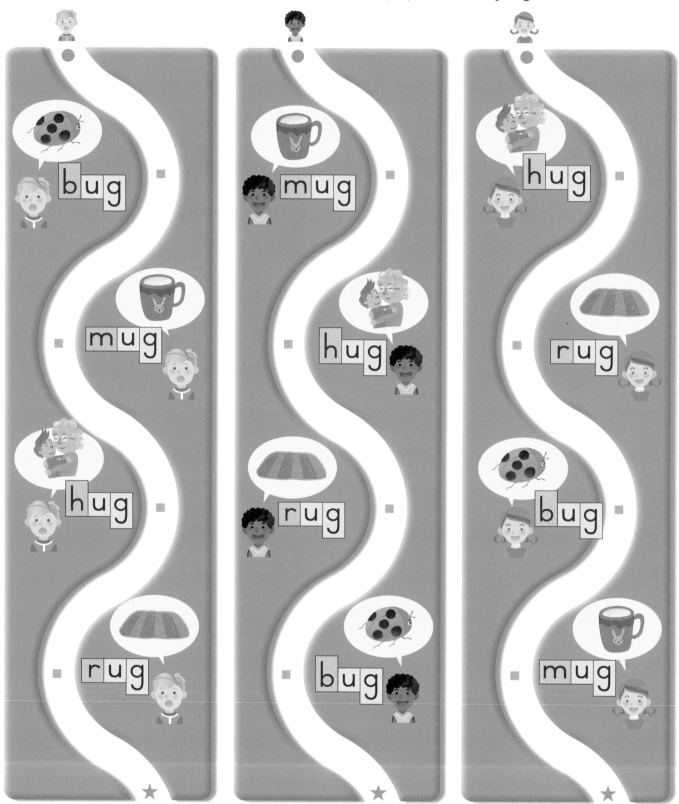

Rhyming Words

Writing "_ug" Words

Name

Date

■ Say the word. Then say the sound of each letter as you trace it.

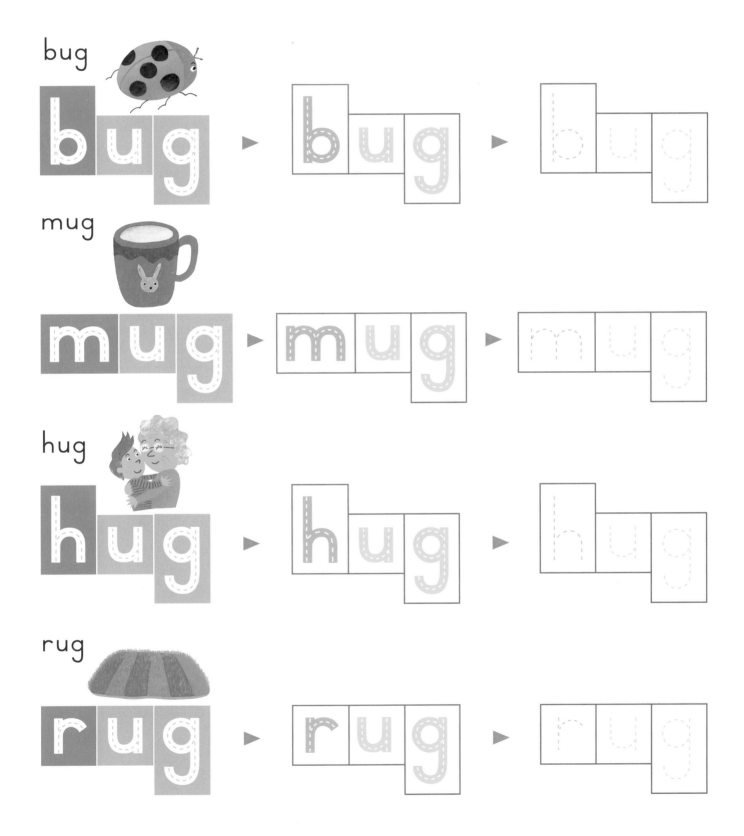

bug

mug

hug

rug

Writing "_ug" Words

■ Say the word. Then say the sound of each letter as you trace and write it.

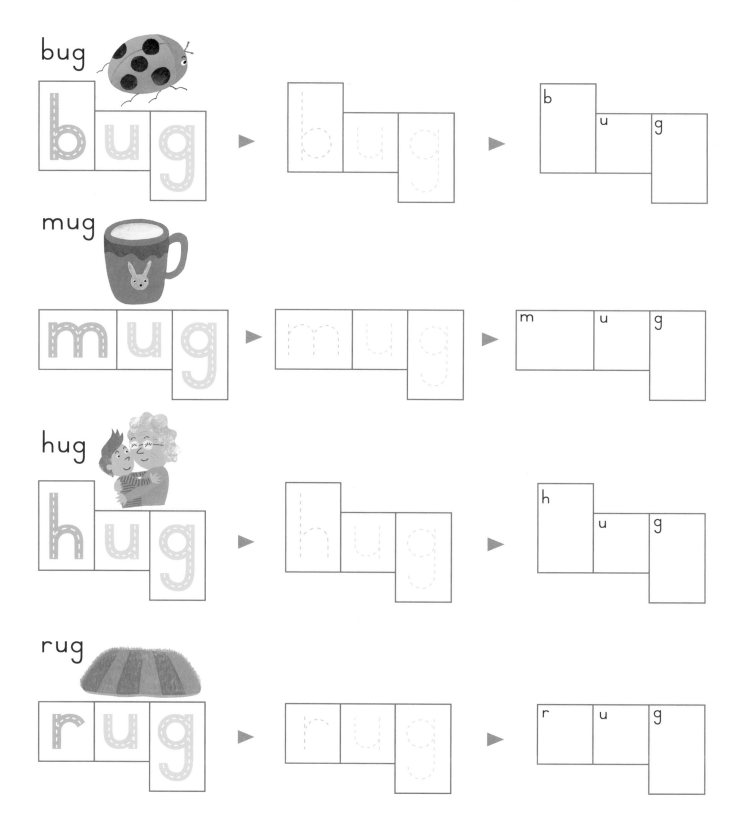

bug

mug

hug

rug

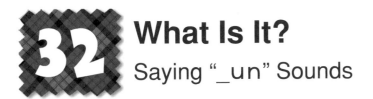

32 What Is It?

Saying "_un" Sounds

Name

Date

■ Match the pictures by drawing a line from the dot (●) to the star (★).

★ **sun**

★ **bun**

★ **run**

★ **fun**

229

Saying "_un" Sounds

■ Draw a line from the dot (●) to the star (★) while saying each word.

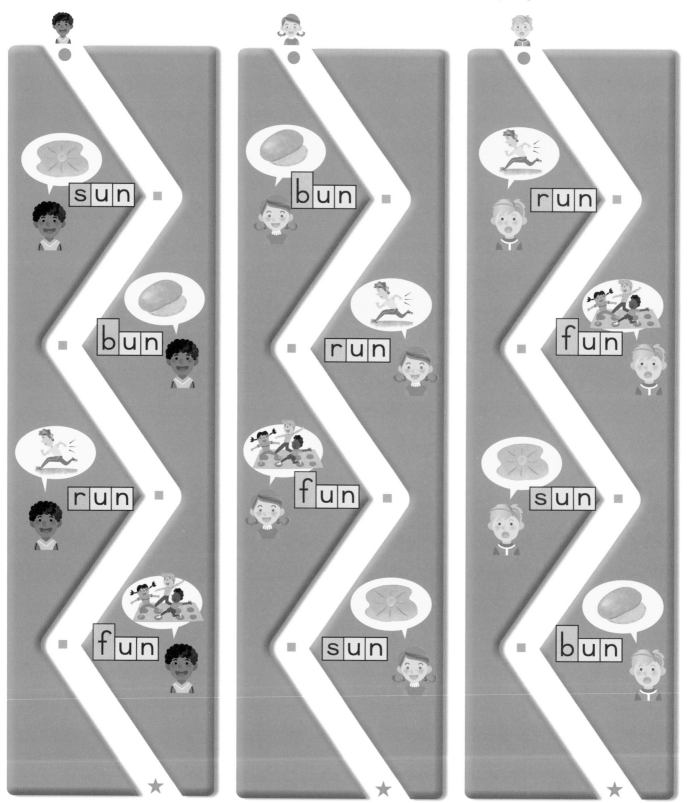

Name

Date

■ Say the word. Then say the sound of each letter as you trace it.

sun

bun

run

fun

Writing "_un" Words

■ Say the word. Then say the sound of each letter as you trace and write it.

sun

bun

run

fun

Review

Saying "_ug" and "_un" Words

■ Draw a line from 🧒 to 🧒 while saying each "_ug" word.
Draw a line from 🧒 to 🧒 while saying each "_un" word.

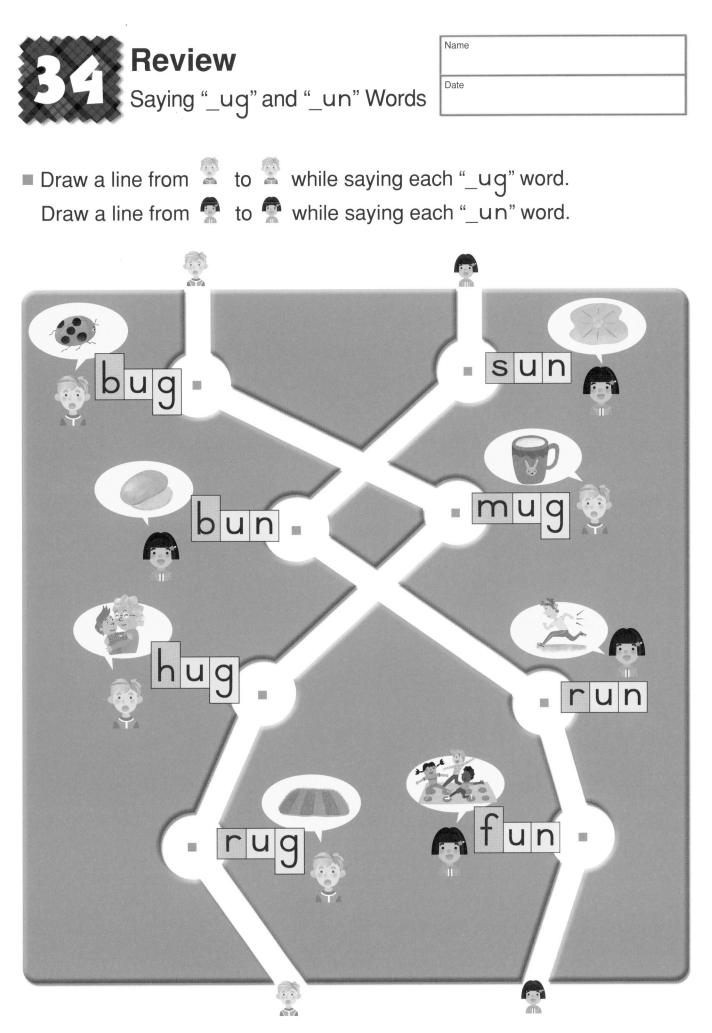

Writing "_ug" and "_un" Words

■ Say the word. Then say the sound of each letter as you write it.

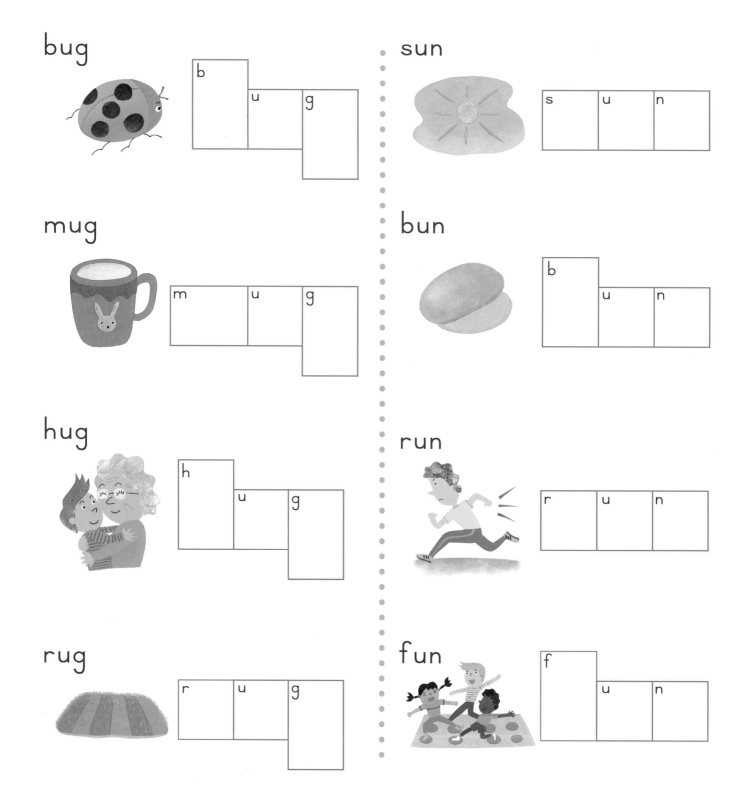

bug

b		
	u	
		g

sun

| s | u | n |

mug

| m | u | g |

bun

| b | | |
| | u | n |

hug

h		
	u	
		g

run

| r | u | n |

rug

| r | u | g |

fun

| f | | |
| | u | n |

Name

Date

To parents
Your child should connect the "rat" to the "cat" again to begin another sequence. Make sure your child draws vertical or horizontal lines, not diagonal ones.

■ Draw a line from the arrow (→) to the star (★), connecting cat to bat to hat to rat while you say the words.

235

Writing "_at" and "_an" Words

■ Say the word. Then say the sound of each letter as you write it.

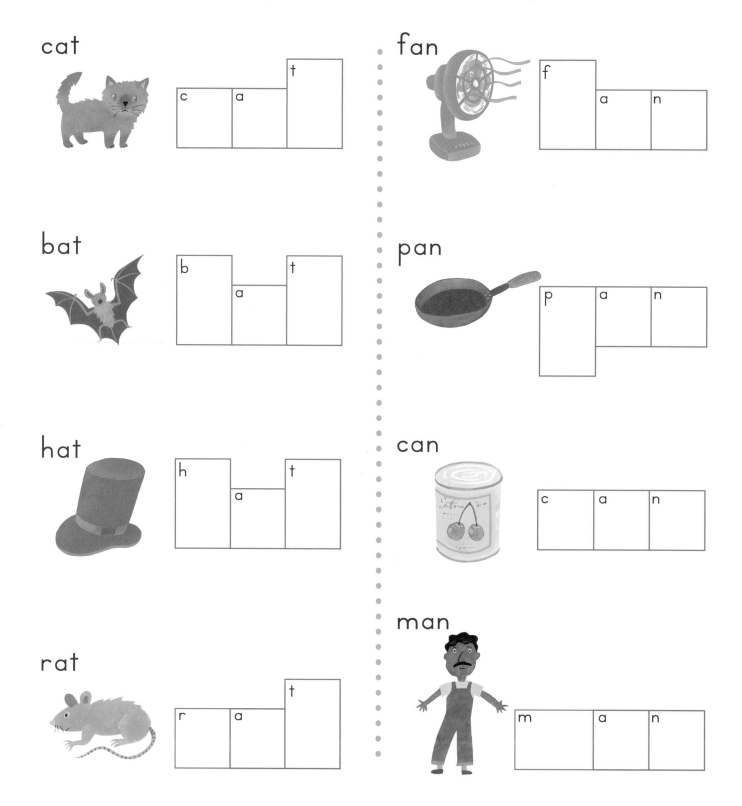

cat

| c | a | t |

fan

| f | a | n |

bat

| b | a | t |

pan

| p | a | n |

hat

| h | a | t |

can

| c | a | n |

rat

| r | a | t |

man

| m | a | n |

Name

Date

To parents
Your child should connect the "tap" to the "cap" again to begin another sequence. Make sure your child draws vertical or horizontal lines, not diagonal ones.

■ Draw a line from the arrow (→) to the star (★), connecting cap to map to nap to tap while you say the words.

cap   map   nap   tap

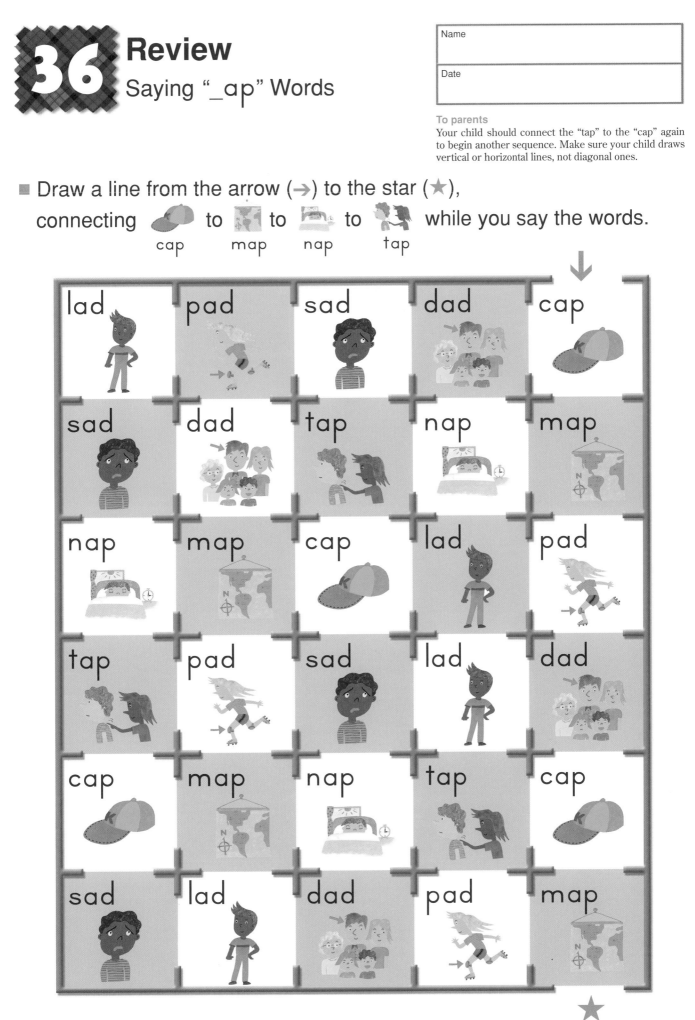

237

Writing "_ap" and "_ad" Words

■ Say the word. Then say the sound of each letter as you write it.

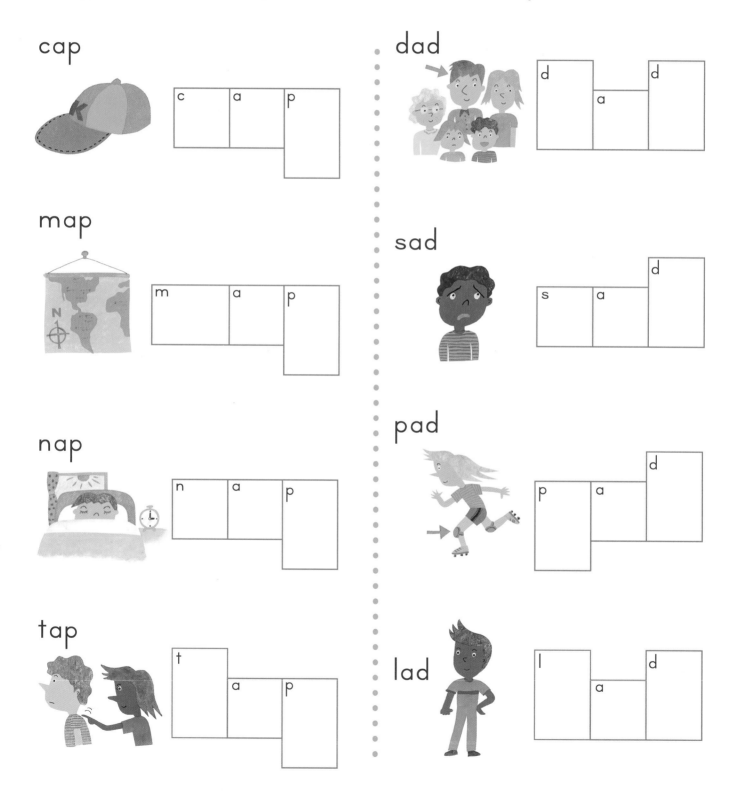

cap

c | a | p

dad

d | | d
| a |

map

m | a | p

sad

| | d
s | a |

nap

n | a | p

pad

| | d
p | a |

tap

t |
| a | p

lad

l | | d
| a |

Name

Date

To parents
Your child should connect the "ten" to the "pen" again to begin another sequence. Make sure your child draws vertical or horizontal lines, not diagonal ones.

■ Draw a line from the arrow (→) to the star (★), connecting 🖊 to 👥 to 🐔 to 🔟 while you say the words.

pen   men   hen   ten

pen	ten 10	hen	men	pen
men	wet	get	pet	net
hen	ten 10	pen	men	wet
net	get	net	hen	pet
hen	pet	get	ten 10	pen
pet	wet	men	net	men

★

239

Writing "_en" and "_et" Words

■ Say the word. Then say the sound of each letter as you write it.

pen

| p | e | n |

net

| n | e | t |

men

| m | e | n |

wet

| w | e | t |

hen

| h | e | n |

pet

| p | e | t |

ten

| t | e | n |

get

| g | e | t |

38 Review

Saying "_in" Words

Name

Date

To parents
Your child should connect the "fin" to the "bin" again to begin another sequence. Make sure your child draws vertical or horizontal lines, not diagonal ones.

■ Draw a line from the arrow (→) to the star (★), connecting 🗑 to 🥫 to 🧷 to 🐟 while you say the words.

bin   tin   pin   fin

zip	lip	hip	tin	bin
rip	bin	fin	pin	rip
zip	tin	zip	hip	lip
hip	pin	fin	bin	tin
bin	lip	rip	hip	pin
rip	pin	zip	lip	fin

★

241

Writing "_in" and "_ip" Words

■ Say the word. Then say the sound of each letter as you write it.

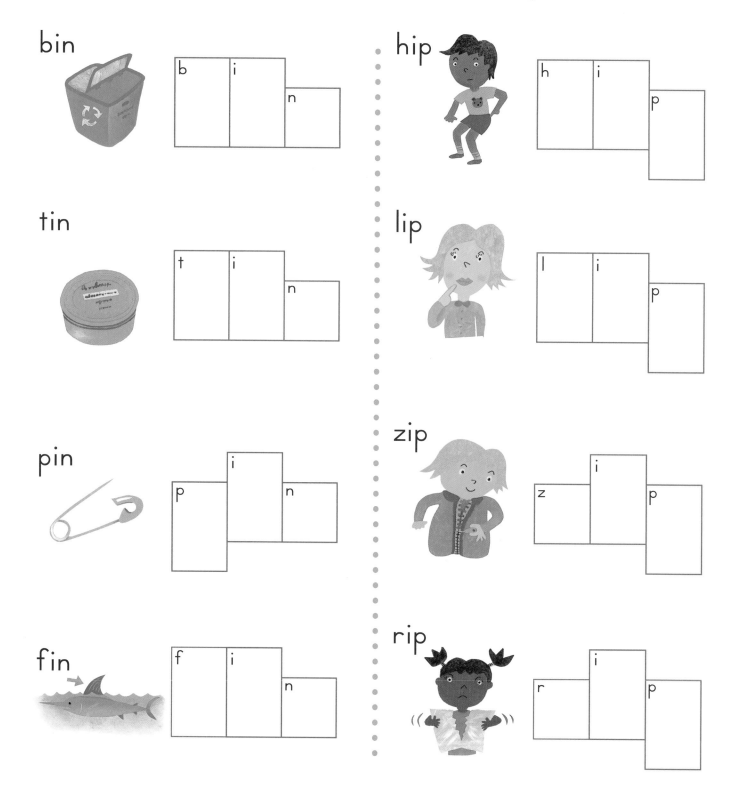

bin

| b | i | |
| | | n |

hip

| h | i | |
| | | p |

tin

| t | i | |
| | | n |

lip

| l | i | |
| | | p |

pin

| | i | |
| p | | n |

zip

| | i | |
| z | | p |

fin

| f | i | |
| | | n |

rip

| | i | |
| r | | p |

Saying "_op" Words

Name

Date

To parents
Your child should connect the "pop" to the "mop" again to begin another sequence. Make sure your child draws vertical or horizontal lines, not diagonal ones.

■ Draw a line from the arrow (→) to the star (★),
   connecting [mop] to [top] to [hop] to [pop] while you say the words.

mop   top   hop   pop

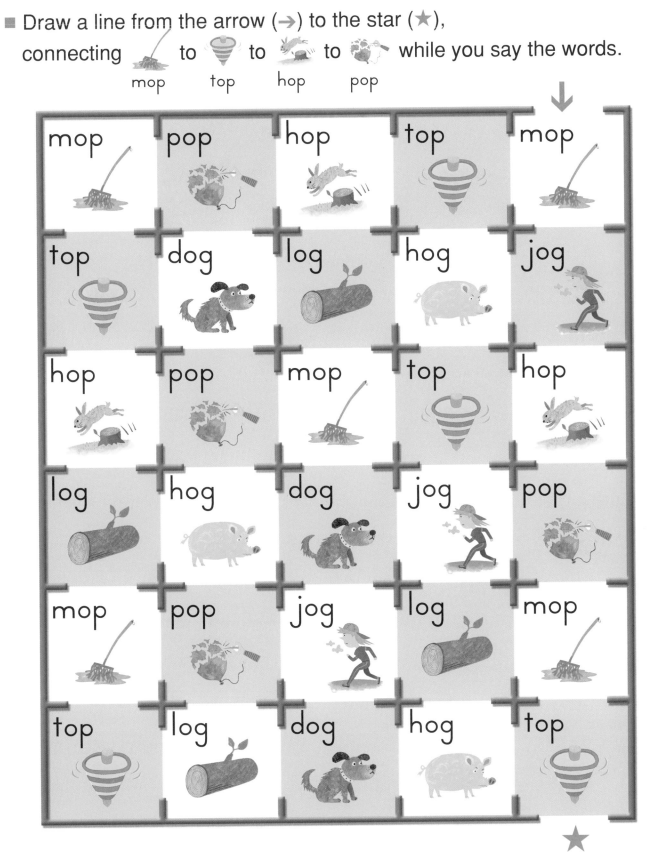

Writing "_op" and "_og" Words

■ Say the word. Then say the sound of each letter as you write it.

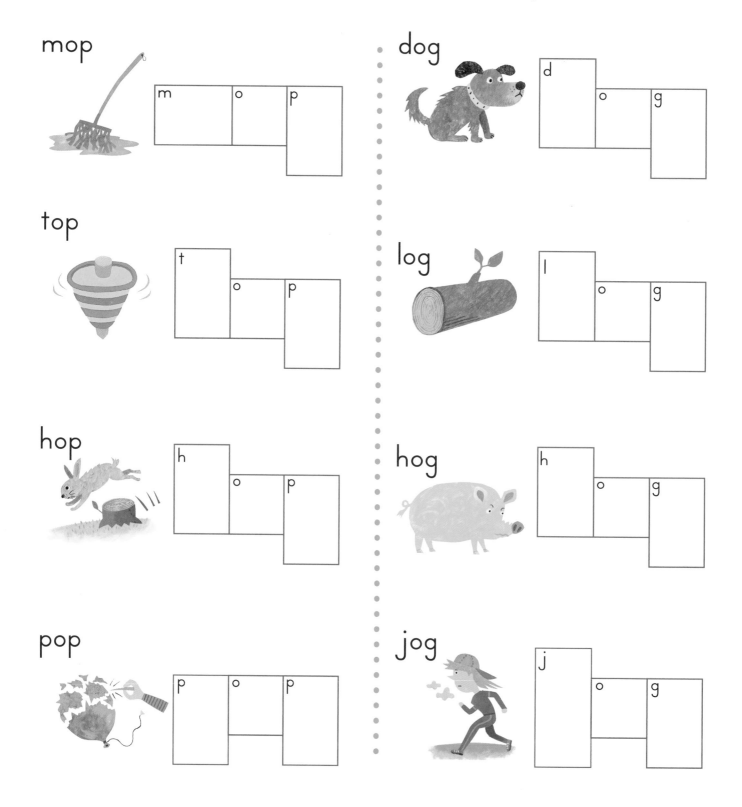

mop

top

hop

pop

dog

log

hog

jog

40 Review

Saying "_ug" Words

Name

Date

To parents
Your child should connect the "rug" to the "bug" again to begin another sequence. Make sure your child draws vertical or horizontal lines, not diagonal ones.

■ Draw a line from the arrow (→) to the star (★),
  connecting 🐞 to 🥛 to 🤗 to 🛝 while you say the words.
  bug   mug   hug   rug

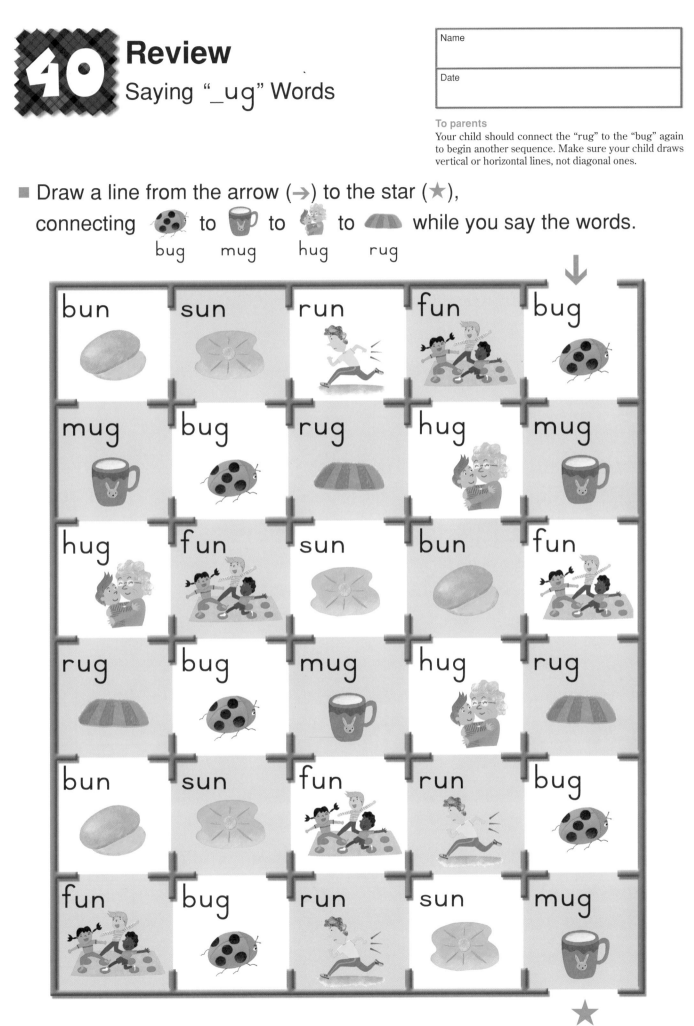

245

Writing "_ug" and "_un" Words

To parents
Your child has been developing phonemic awareness skills, which are necessary building blocks to learning how to sound out words and to read. Please encourage your child and nurture a lifelong love of reading.

■ Say the word. Then say the sound of each letter as you write it.

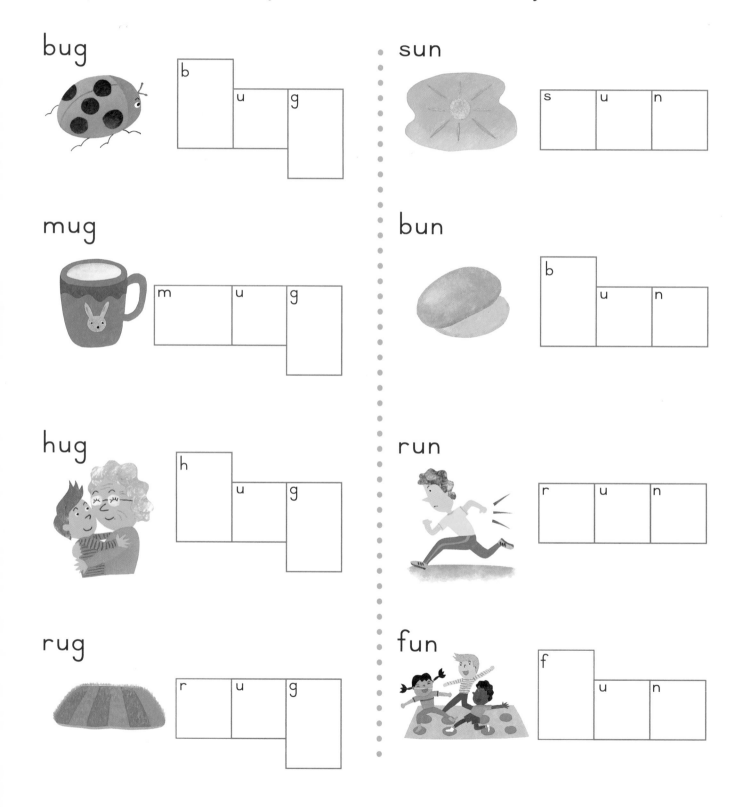

bug

b | u | g

sun

s | u | n

mug

m | u | g

bun

b | u | n

hug

h | u | g

run

r | u | n

rug

r | u | g

fun

f | u | n

Certificate of

Achievement

....

is hereby congratulated on completing

My Big Book of
NUMBERS, LETTERS & WORDS

Presented on .... , 20 ....

....

Parent or Guardian